THE TRUE MEANING OF LIFE

BY

JUDITH HINDLE

Copyright © 2018 Judith Hindle

The right of Judith Hindle to be the author of this work has Been asserted in accordance with the Copyright, Designs and Patents Act 1988.

This is a first edition publishing through KDP and all rights remain with the author Judith Hindle. First published in 2018.

No part of this publication may be reproduced, stored or transmitted in any form or by any means without prior written consent from the Author. No part of the cover design may be copied or reproduced without prior written consent of the designer Steven Lacey. www.anclaro.com

A CIP catalogue for this book is available from the British Library.

Production by Steven Lacey at www.anclaro.com

Edited & Typeset by Sasi Langford & New Age Publishing & Events.

DEDICATION

This book is dedicated to my two beautiful sons who make my physical life a joy to behold, as they have chosen me as their mother in their incarnations which has been an honour from the day they were born and every day since.

To my 'soul connection' Jay, who loves me unconditionally for all my faults and has supported me through this long, arduous journey, and with whom I have shared many lives.

Last, but by no means least, I dedicate this book in loving memory of my Mum & Dad, Patricia and Richard Miller.

Contents

AUTHOR'S NOTE 6
THANKS & ACKNOWLEDGEMENTS 8
INTRODUCTION 10
HOW WE ARE CREATED 14
WHERE DOES IT ALL BEGIN? 19
WE ARE BORN AND WE GROW 29
WE START TO WAKE UP 35
THE CIRCLE OF LIFE 41
WHAT REALLY HAPPENS WHEN WE DIE? 47
DO GHOSTS AND SPIRITS EXIST? 52
WHO CAN COMMUNICATE WITH SPIRIT? 57
NO ROYAL BOX: LIFE IN SPIRIT WORLD 62
THE AKASHIC RECORDS & PAST LIVES 76
LESSONS AND DESTINY 86
GOD AND RELIGION 94
WHO HAS THE ANSWERS? 100
THE NEW AGE 105
OTHER DIMENSIONS 112
THE MIND, BODY AND HOLISTIC HEALING 115
HOW CAN WE HELP OURSELVES? 132
THE LAW OF ATTRACTION 138

YOUR FUTURE IS UP TO YOU 149
A LAST MESSAGE FROM SPIRIT...154
CLEANSING AND PROTECTING GUIDE 159
MEET YOUR SPIRIT GUIDE MEDITATION........................161

AUTHOR'S NOTE

Writing this book has been very difficult for me as well as spiritually enlightening. I started this book at the beginning of 2013, completed it in July 2015, and I am now having it published in 2018. The way I believed things to be when I started writing this book has drastically changed to how I feel now. I believe Spirit gave me this challenge for my own awakening and realisations as well as for all those who will read this book. I have certainly come a long way during the writing of this book.

When I first became a Medium and therapist I wanted to change the world and help everyone. I became so despondent and disillusioned with life in general and my own life, when I realised that I could not come to everybody's aid. I did not believe that anyone should suffer or experience trauma or abuse etc., I raged against all that is wrong in our world and forgot to focus on what is good. I fought against my gift and my Spirit Guides, including Lazarus, again and again. I gave up helping people, but invariably when someone rang me in genuine need I just could not say no.

What I understand now, after all I have learned during the writing of this book, and with my communication with Spirit World, is that I cannot help everyone. In fact, it is not my place to even try. I can only help those who genuinely want help or want to change because they no longer want the hardships they have been living through. I have come to realise that I have evolved and progressed to a much higher level now from where

I first started in 2005 and my knowledge is constantly growing. During the last three years I have struggled to find a place where I can fit in, where people will listen and consider what Spirit say through me, without all the negative beliefs and judgement. What I can do is not 'fortune telling' or some form of gimmick, it is a connection to my 'Higher Self' and the 'Living Energy' of the universe, some may call it 'God' or 'Source'. In a world of labels, I have to use the one that people can understand and relate to, although it is tarnished with those that are fake and who abuse peoples' vulnerability, although Spirit are steadily weeding these types of people out. All the answers we ever require for anything are always within ourselves, my work with Spirit is changing, my focus is now to work with Spirit but in a much more constructive way that helps people like you all around the world connect to your living spiritual energy, and to eliminate your negativity from the root causes, which will allow you to be happy and fulfilled in your earthly life and beyond.

J.H, March 2018

THANKS & ACKNOWLEDGEMENTS

My first thanks are dedicated to Spirit World as without my connection to them everything I have experienced and learned would never have been possible. I want to sincerely thank Mary Holt, Author of 'Spirituality Matters', whom without I would never have even known I was a Medium, never mind become one.

I would like to thank Sasi Langford for all her help in editing and putting this book together, so it is fit for purpose! I want to thank my friend Alan Whitehead for putting me in touch with Sasi in the first place and for all our soul-searching conversations and insights and to Steven Lacey, (www.anclaro.com) my technical 'Angel' who produced the cover for this book, and helps with all my marketing, web design and everything else!

I would also like to thank all the important people in my life that make up my friends and family in this lifetime. There are too many of you to mention and I do not want to offend anyone by leaving you out, so this is dedicated to you all with love and thanks for all your support over the years.

All my love

Jude xx

INTRODUCTION

In January 2015, just as I was putting the finishing touches to this book, my father passed away. He had Alzheimer's for nine years, and was in a nursing home, and if you have experienced this yourself, you will know that you lose the real person long before their physical body dies. Dad's illness taught me a lot about this condition, because I learned that it's not only a person's mind that is affected. In the same way that skin cancer enters the body to destroy it from the inside out, so does Alzheimer's. As the mind deteriorates it can also shut down different bodily functions: in Dad's case, he lost the ability to swallow and was on a pureed diet, but I didn't realise this until he broke his hip in January and ended up in the hospital. I knew from the moment I got the phone call saying he had a broken hip, and needed an operation, that he was not coming out again. When you are connected to Spirit, you get a 'knowing' about things, which is both a blessing and a curse, because sometimes that knowledge will be deeply upsetting for you.

Dad never really recovered from the operation, his blood pressure would not come back up and he would not eat or drink. When he tried to drink, he would choke, and this is how we found out that his swallow reflex had gone completely. It was no coincidence that this experience had happened to me just as this book was nearing completion, because I have experienced many of the situations mentioned in this book first-hand. I know this was sent to give me the final proof needed to confirm what Spirit has said to me during my work with them, is the absolute truth.

A couple of days after Dad's operation he started speaking to people who were not there, but he was not suffering from delirium as he was interacting with those around him too. I felt my Grandmother, Grandfather and my Uncle Len around my Dad, but then that's only to be expected. I knew they had come for him as all our loved ones do. On the Saturday night I had a twenty-five-minute conversation with my Dad's mother, whom I had never met on the Earth plane. She told me many things, including the day my Dad would pass away, which she said would be the following Wednesday.

The next day, Sunday, I had to make the decision to put Dad on the 'Pathway'. This is where they withdraw all fluids and medication apart from pain relief until the person dies. This is the singularly most difficult decision I have ever had to make, and for someone like me who is connected to Spirit, I felt like I was playing God. He had developed pneumonia from his own saliva as it was going in to his chest cavity instead of where it should have, because his swallow reflex had gone. I knew beyond a shadow of a doubt he was suffering, yet it did not make the decision any easier.

I stayed with him and watched him battle against death, because he had done things in his life that had hurt others, and I saw first-hand how those who are scared to pass over prolong their own suffering. I reassured him that his loved ones were there, and everything would be okay. I thought my Grandmother was wrong because he kept going all through Wednesday, but then at about 8pm his breathing started to change. All the lights in the room began flickering on and off continually, and then I knew his time had come, because I could feel those that had come for him.

As I looked above Dad's head I could see a wispy, silver smoke-like apparition, swirling upwards, and I knew this was the ethereal part of him starting to leave. It was painful to sit with Dad who was dying physically, yet spiritually it was the most amazing experience of my life, because I witnessed what others had told me about, and in those final moments the whole thing became crystal clear. Finally, Dad stopped breathing gently, and quietly slipped away. I will never forget the peace that settled over his face, nor will I ever forget the overwhelming feeling of love in that room. I cannot describe the strength of the energy in the room as my Dad passed over into Spirit, and as I write this now I am welling up with tears from the force of the feeling that enveloped me as they came to take him home.

When my turn comes to leave this mortal coil, I will greet death like an old friend as it is only death of the physical body, not of the eternal soul. Even though I miss Dad's physical presence, I know he lives on, out of the earthly suffering that he experienced, and I know that I was meant to witness it for my own progression and understanding. My job now is to teach all those who will listen about Spirit World and the 'True' meaning of life.

Love to all living species within this world.

Judith x

~When every animal, plant and flower has vanished from the world, then perhaps Man will realise that he cannot eat money~

HOW WE ARE CREATED

The Earth was created over billions of years, and both theological and Darwinian evolutionary explanations are correct in their own ways. The universe and planets were created by physical manifestations of atoms and energy evolving over billions of years, and from a collective consciousness of energy that we would term 'God', 'The Creator' or whatever name you choose to call it. I am not a scientist, and the object of this book is not to delve in to the 'How' of creation, but more of the 'Why'.

When we incarnate into human form, we consist of both energy and matter, but when we return to spirit we are only energy. The human body is merely a vehicle for our soul to travel in, a shell, and in the same way that a car body is nothing without its engine, the human body is nothing without its soul and mind energy. The physical body is matter, the soul and mind are energy. All our bodily organs, the brain, skeleton, skin, blood cells and eyes are physical matter, and although the heart can continue beating after a person is 'brain dead', once their mind energy has ceased to function any living being is clinically dead.

All living species, in fact, the entire universe, function and exists because of energy. Yet, even though we are all part of the living whole and could not exist as humans without our animal and plant species, we seem intent on destroying them. Animals have souls and mind energy, the same as we do. Plants have pain receptors and owe their existence to energy also. Humankind is connected to every other living species on the planet and we should be doing our utmost to protect and conserve them.

A human being cannot function without its life force energy. We are the most intelligent and complex of all the species on the Earth plane, but many of us still do not appreciate this fact. We use our mind energy to invent and create, to rationalise and problem solve, but an animal will merely follow its primal instincts. It eats, sleeps, reproduces, hunts for what it needs, protects its young, and finds shelter, but what their minds' lack are the thought processes that would allow it to formulate its actions. An animal is not intelligent enough to make informed choices, but we are. How many of us use this wonderful power and freedom we have above other species effectively and correctly? How many of us use it for greed and selfishness, and how many use it for good and selflessness?

Imagine if we woke up tomorrow and discovered that there were no animals or plants left on Earth. How long do you think it would be before there were no people? If the animals and plants woke up tomorrow and there were no humans left, how do you think they would fare? They would thrive and survive as there would be no humans poaching the animals or destroying their environment. We need animals and plants for our continuing existence so instead of harming them we need to wake up now and protect them with every ounce of our being. We must fully appreciate and understand their vital necessity to us humans on the Earth plane. The animal and plant kingdoms do not need us at all to survive, but we need them – so who is the superior species now? What if I told you that the honey bee is singularly the most important insect on the planet and crucial for our continued survival? Honey bees are responsible for pollinating about three-quarters of the world's agricultural crops, yet their numbers are rapidly decreasing due to our use of pesticides. Humans need to start putting their notions of superiority and ego to one side, and realise what is *really* important, if they want future generations to survive.

When the Earth was created, everything needed for survival was provided, but so many of us still do not comprehend the magic and magnificence of the resources we have access to here on Earth. Beautiful crystal-clear water, which is the most vital thing for all living things to survive and allows all manner of species to grow and be hydrated. There are enough food sources for all of us, no matter if you are a carnivore, omnivore or herbivore. We have trees that not only oxygenate our planet but provide food for all manner of insect and animal life, as well as being made from a substance that humans can construct shelter from and from which I can print this book! The beauty and complexity of the Polar opposites which control our sea levels and the power of natural disasters that the Earth undergoes, which makes room for new life to spring from, such as the fires on the plains of the Savannah, are truly things to be marvelled at.

Have you ever appreciated the miracle of self? The perfect creation that is the human being? Stop for a minute and think about the human body: the networks of veins and capillaries that keep our blood flowing, all the organs that keep us alive without us even consciously thinking about what functions they perform or indeed *how* they do it. Think of the complexity of the most powerful tool on the planet: the human brain. All its synapses, cells, electrical pulses, waves and nerves work in the background, providing us with memory, thought and problem-solving abilities, and endless more amazing powers.

We just take it all for granted until the body becomes sick in some way because of the way we treat or neglect it. Then we start to realise how fragile life can really be. The human body is so remarkable that we can smoke, ingest drugs, drink alcohol, feed it all manner of man-made chemicals and yet it survives our mistreatment! Do you realise just how magnificent that really is? It is only after long term abuse that the body starts to break down and all the damage we have inflicted upon it starts to take effect. The human body was designed to last hundreds, if not thousands of years originally, but because of so called progress, some of the things that we have invented to make our life more pleasurable in some way, actually end our life span a lot sooner than was ever intended.

If you could look inside yourself and fully appreciate the walking miracle of life that you are, indeed that *all* living species are, and to respect your body accordingly, then not only would you be more healthy and happy as an individual, the whole world would become more balanced too.

~It is not our beginnings that makes us who we are, but our choices~

WHERE DOES IT ALL BEGIN?

When in Spirit form we are all pure energy, not requiring a physical form as we do on the Earth plane, because there is no need for physical manifestation. When a spirit returns to the Earth plane it forms a physical being once more. When I talk about an individual's 'Spirit' it is only another term for 'Soul' which is the same thing. Many babies are classed as 'Old Souls' which simply means that they have been incarnated many times on the Earth plane already. How many times have you looked into a new born baby's eyes and felt that they have been here before?

There are many different levels in the Spirit dimension, or Heaven, if you prefer that terminology, because they are both essentially the same thing. Before we return to the Earth plane we 'choose' our parents, our gender, our colour, our race, and our lessons. We also choose our destiny in that lifetime, whether we will be rich or poor, healthy or disabled in some way, whether we will have a long incarnation or a short one, and whether we will be a head of state or a goat herder, we choose it all. Many of you will protest this with every fibre of your being, just as I did on my path to realisation. Why would we ask for such horrific things to happen to us? Why would we choose to have abusive people in our lives? Who in their right mind would ask for the lives they have had, when they have experienced trauma and unhappiness? The answer is in the question…*for the experience.*

For the soul to be whole and fully progressed it needs to have experienced every facet of life. It needs to have been cruel and kind, rich and poor, different nationalities, different religions, to have been the abused and the abuser, the loved and unloved, criminal and law abiding, healthy and sick, intelligent and non-intelligent – the list is almost endless. As you can imagine this can take many lifetimes to achieve. Some souls, when they return to 'Spirit', decide they have had enough and stay there, whereas others like me seem to be gluttons for punishment and keep coming back for more experiences. The more progressed your soul is when you go back to Spirit, the higher the realm you will return to, and when all your learning cycles are complete then you will remain in Spirit to teach and guide others.

There are many guardians in Spirit. We are each assigned a guardian angel at birth, and whether you believe this or not makes no difference, as you cannot alter that fact. Our guardian is there to gently, or forcefully sometimes, guide us through our life and to nudge us back on our path if we have gone astray. They will put thoughts in our head, open doors of opportunity, put obstacles in our way if something is not the right time for us, and save our life if is not our time to return to Spirit. If you disbelieve this just think back, have you ever survived an accident that you should not have or had a near miss? Has an opportunity presented itself to you at just the right time? Have you had a health issue that was treated just in time, or one that you survived but you do not know how? Many people put these things down to 'Coincidence' or 'Luck' when in fact there is no such thing, everything happens for a reason, even if that reason is not clear at the time.

Think back to a difficult time in your life, and now think of where you are now in your life. I guarantee that even though you may still not understand why that difficult experience happened to you, you will have learnt something from it, or have become a better or wiser person than you were then. We spend so much time resenting and being bitter about negative experiences in our past, we forget to focus on the lessons from them and where we are now. People spend so much time reliving the past or worrying about the future that they forget to live in the here and now, in the present. We cannot change the past, only learn from the experiences, we cannot know the future, so worrying about it is pointless, we can and should live only in the present, and learn to appreciate what we have got, and not what we think we should have.

How many of us right now feel we are unhappy with our life in some way? Do you feel your life is on a one-way ticket downhill? Does every day seem like a struggle? Is there some area of your life that particularly disheartens you, for example work, relationships, health? Do you keep repeating negative patterns in your life? Have you ever asked the question: "Why

Me?" What if I told you that the power to change all that lies entirely with you? Would you believe me if I told you that you asked for certain challenges before you were even born? Would you believe me I wonder, if I said you are exactly where you should be right now at this time in your life, and where you go from now is only up to you, and that no one is to blame for whatever you feel is wrong in your life, only you.

It is very difficult to realise that we are the product of our own choices and to fully accept responsibility – it took me many years and I am still on that path of realisation. There are times when I question and fight against it, but then things go wrong, and I have to hold the mirror up, taking a good look in again. When we are children we are at the mercy of our elders, however once we have grown we are at the mercy of ourselves and keep ourselves imprisoned in our vicious circle of negative thought, behaviours and actions when we hold the key to freedom the whole time.

We look to others to make our life better, we go from relationship to relationship, job to job, interest to interest, trying to find something or someone that will fill our gap and make us whole. When they, or it, cannot fill that void, we move on again. What we must realise, is that nothing and nobody can live up to such a tall order. It is an impossible task. The filling of the gap must come from within yourself, no one person and no one thing can fulfil you or make you happy, only yourself, and the day you realise this is the day you take back control of your own life.

If you are not happy with an aspect of your life, stop focusing on the negative part of it and start changing it. The human race is very good at blaming others for its misfortunes, when in fact it is our own thought processes and the way we react to situations that keep us imprisoned. Although we cannot control other's damaging thoughts, deeds, actions or behaviours, we can control the way *we* allow it to affect us. If you were to strip yourself back and peel away the layers like an onion, can you say with complete and utter honesty that where you are in life right now is totally someone else's fault and that you have not made any wrong decisions or choices, or had a negative mentality that has contributed to where you find yourself now?

During our lifetime on Earth, we will have many challenges to overcome: loss, grief, abuse, heartbreak, financial worries, sickness, accidents and trauma to name but a few. These things are *real*, and I am not saying that when we are going through these events that we should not let it affect us and be jolly and happy under the circumstances. Grief, for example, is a process that must be undergone, but how we allow these things to influence our future is something that you can control. Believe me, I do not speak of these things lightly, as I have been through much trauma during my childhood and life, and although we cannot control what influences us in our early years, we can choose how to deal with any negative effects when we become adults.

It is not our beginnings that make us who we are, but our choices and reactions to negativity. Once you understand and embrace the true meaning of life, the reasons why we have negative challenges to overcome will become clear. Great oak trees come from baby acorns, one step at a time and with positive attitude will come positive change, I guarantee it.

Before we come back to the Earth plane we make a contract with our 'Higher Masters' in the Spirit dimension, choosing what lessons we wish to learn during this incarnation and sometimes if we have not learnt our lessons or 'Karma' from a previous lifetime, we have to come back and do it all again. The term karma comes from the Sanskrit word for 'action' or 'deed' and is rather like a cosmic sum, or weighing up, of your actions in this life that can influence your future. You could also think of it as your lessons of destiny, and try as you might, you cannot change something that is your destiny. However, even though our fundamental lessons are prearranged before we return to the Earth plane, our individual choices play a great part in how slowly or quickly we achieve them. Our individual choices also play a part in whom we allow to interact with us in our lives along our path. It is said that all roads lead to Rome, and so too all paths will lead to your final destiny. You will learn your lessons during your incarnation on Earth, (or not, and have to come and do it again) but how rough or smooth the journey to Spirit is depends mainly on your choices.

Let me explain what I mean by choice, which is also termed 'Free Will'. Human beings are given the gift of free will before they are created, so they can experience all they want and need to experience in their individual lifetimes. The old saying, 'You only learn from your mistakes' is fundamental in your life lessons. Even though your soul contract is drawn up and you are incarnated to learn certain things in this lifetime, whether you do that or not is your choice. Every person has two paths they can take at any one time, or about any decision on their life journey. The path or decision they make is what alters their outcome or their level of happiness or makes their road rough or smooth. Let me give you an example.

Someone's life lesson may be to overcome abuse. So, for arguments sake, let's say a soul is incarnated as a female and she falls in love with a gorgeous man whom she absolutely adores. Over time, she sees flashes of aggression in this person, which gives her a bad gut feeling, however she ignores it because she loves him, but it still makes her uneasy. Then one day 'Bam!' he assaults her. She is shocked and upset but gives him another chance, and invariably he does it again. Now, this is where choice comes in: she can choose to stay and allow him to do it for the next twenty years or until he kills her, or she can leave now. Whether she has been abused just once or a hundred times, she has still learnt the lesson, and this is where her choice of paths present themselves. If she stays she could end up going back to Spirit before her time, or she could put up with being treated like that for the rest of her physical life. Alternatively, if she chooses to leave she may end up being blissfully happy, or at the very least, she has saved her own life because she chose another path. This may seem harsh, but it is true.

Many people go back to Spirit before they should or endure terrible experiences because they do not listen to their gut instinct or they simply make the wrong choices. However, if it is a soul's time to return to the Spirit dimension then circumstance will work against them and they will return, but it is all part of our life's lessons. As I said earlier, we all have a pre-approved soul contract before we reincarnate on the Earth plane, and part of that agreement is the biological age that we will reach before returning home to Spirit once more. This length of time, however, can be extended while we are here if we have not quite learnt what we needed to or still have obligations to fulfil. If it really is your time, whether you are two minutes old, two weeks, months, years or a hundred years old matters not, then your physical body will die.

People have survived things that they really should not have, and we often call that a 'miracle', but the reason they survived what should have been a fatal episode is because it was not their time. There was a man in Australia who jumped out of a plane and his parachute failed to open. He fell three thousand feet through the air, landed in bushes and his only injury was a broken ankle. Yet you can fall three feet from a ladder whilst painting the ceiling in your home and break your neck! When it is your time it is your time, and nothing can be done about it. Age is a manmade thing, the same as time, and because of this we believe if a person is too young to die in our perception of age and time, then we perceive this as a tragedy and we become very angry and bitter. Of course, when we love someone, and they die, especially when it is a child, we cannot comprehend how we can outlive them when they have their whole lives in front of them. If you understand that age is manmade and only a number, and that the destiny of that soul may only have been to have incarnated for a short period of time, even if you do not agree with it, then the meaning of life becomes clearer. A child who passes back to Spirit very early, or children born with an illness or disabilities have chosen that for a specific reason, and sometimes the lessons are not for the children but for the families they are born into. I will explain more about this later.

I believe a couple of my life lessons must be forgiveness and patience, because life has thrown people into my path who have hurt me terribly, whom I have had to learn to forgive, and also, I struggle with being patient. I believe I was given the gift of clairvoyance to teach me many lessons upon this Earth plane in this lifetime, and to share this knowledge with others.

Choice, as well as pre-determined life lessons, are what shape and make us as a person, as it develops our soul and our mind energy. They say the more hardship and challenges you have during your lifetime, the faster your soul progresses, and with that comes understanding which you bring back again and again. Your soul is made up of every lifetime you have experienced thus far, and it is what makes you who you are, making up the very essence of your spiritual being, for we are all spiritual beings in a human vehicle. You can also bring negative karma over from a previous lifetime, as well as the learnings. In my work I have discovered when using regression therapy to treat clients with depression or problems in their current lives, that the root cause comes from a past life, which they spontaneously regress back to when we are looking for the root cause. This is also very true of phobias and irrational fears, I had a client who was petrified of driving on the motorway and being near lorries, when I regressed her, she had been a male lorry driver in a previous life and killed a lot of people when he had a heart attack at the wheel and crashed the lorry. Once I took her through the lessons and got her to release the negative emotions connected to that life, she was fine driving on the motorway after that. Regression therapy is an amazing way of helping you with negative emotions and responses you have brought with you in to this life, and to help eliminate negative karma.

~Our children are only ever on loan to us, from the moment they are born they are their own person on their own individual journey~

WE ARE BORN AND WE GROW

As I said earlier, we choose who our parents are going to be before we are born. I know some will find this very difficult to believe or understand if, like me, you had a challenging childhood. When we are infants we are at the mercy of our parents, siblings, other adults and surroundings and even though we choose our parents for the certain lessons they can teach us, we do not always choose how those lessons are learnt or of the outside influences that can affect us.

As children, we have very little power to stop bad things happening to us, and our main imprint years are between the time of birth and seven years old. This is when most of our beliefs and value structures are created, although as an adult we can change this. If a child has suffered a great deal during these years, then this is where mental illness and bad behaviours can come from in later life. Even though we are meant to learn certain lessons we cannot control our childhood, and this is where the people who we encounter can negatively or positively affect our lives. If it is in a negative way, then we can spend much of our life trying to deal with that residual negativity. It is difficult to understand, but I will try to explain it.

The people and outside influences we encounter during our childhood shapes what kind of adult we ourselves become. Outside influences cover a multitude of things including, religion, family, traumatic events, or death. We may have our parents' beliefs instilled in us during our childhood, but as we grow we form our own ideas and beliefs and will sometimes pull away from all that has been ingrained in us. This is our own unseen life path and lessons creeping in again, even though we may not be aware of it.

Many children see spirits and angels because they are still connected to that dimension until they are about eight or nine years old. Depending on their childhood and other influences, they will keep that connection, or they might disconnect for a while, or indeed, for the whole of their incarnation on the Earth plane. Children who have had very challenging childhoods are normally the ones who will have been aware of Spirit or had 'invisible friends' long past the normal age range. All children have the ability to see these spiritual beings, but some will talk about it and others will not. Some children are chastised or even abused for talking about what they can see, so they learn to shut it out, but they become very confused because they know what they can see is real, whereas the adults around them are telling them it is wrong. Some children ask where their 'Other Mummy' is, as they remember past lives.

What parents forget is that all children are on loan to us, they may look like us, share some of our characteristics and our genes, yet from the moment they are born they have their own mind, body, and over time will possess their own views and belief systems. They also have their own souls and their own journey to complete. Therefore, I will never understand why or how parents can mistreat their children. They do not understand that one day their child will grow into an adult, and in most cases become bigger and stronger than the parent that once mistreated them. Children do not stay small and insignificant forever.

As parents, it is our job to love and nurture our children, to respect them and to teach them to respect others, to guide them with principles of right and wrong, but at the same time allow them to question and explore the world around them. We will make mistakes as parents, we are only human and on our own journey, but we too must learn from them and remember that the childhood we give our children will remain with them for the rest of their lives. They will either be balanced and whole individuals or they will be battle weary and scarred – which ones will your children be? Just because we created and gave birth to our children does not give us the right to treat them badly in any way, they are not ours, they are completely their own.

Children who have had traumatic or abusive childhoods, may turn to alcohol or drugs, while some turn to crime and others manage to avoid all these things. It really depends on the environment they are in and who they have in their support network. As a child who lived in and out of children's homes and foster care myself, and having experienced lots of trauma in my childhood, I understand this only too well. I was lucky, I am very strong minded and did not self-medicate to block out what happened to me, however some kids just suffer far too much. Their minds become unable to cope anymore, and this ushers in mental illness, which is why many teenagers take their own lives as they try to cope with depression and the events that have happened to them.

As I've mentioned before, we are here to learn certain lessons, but how we learn them can be out of our control, and this is a perfect illustration of that principle. During our childhood years, the influences and people around us have the control, and if we are fortunate when we reach adulthood we can get professional help to eliminate the negativity of our earlier lives, but again this depends on the strength and determination of the person involved too. Here is that choice thing again! We cannot change the past, but we can change how we allow it to affect us. We can go down the 'Wrong' path or the 'Right' path, some go down the wrong path to start with, but then decide to make their lives better and become a Survivor rather than remaining a Victim. Even though we can be resentful and bitter about our childhood and the bad things that have happened to us, I know if I had not gone through what I did I would not be the compassionate, caring person I am today. The difficult experiences in my life have equipped me to help thousands of people through my work to lead happier, more fulfilled lives. If I had lived a charmed life, I may never have helped all those people.

As we grow we start to learn all about the world around us, through our own eyes and through the opinions and advice of others. We form friendships and relationships outside our own family unit and form our own beliefs, values and opinions. We start to question many things that have been instilled in us from childhood which perhaps do not 'sit' quite right with us anymore. If we are lucky we will experience love and go through our teenage years, into our adult years experiencing and living life to the full or we have struggle and trauma and fight our way into adulthood.

Then finally we have arrived into adulthood where we suddenly are supposed to have all the answers and behave responsibly. If we have children, we are expected to know how to be good parents, perhaps without having had good role models ourselves. As we enter adulthood, if we have had psychic or spiritual experiences when we were younger, and we are meant to be aware of these during this incarnation, then these sensations will start to reappear.

Every single person on this Earth can communicate with the spirit dimension. Every child is still connected until they are about eight or nine years old, and then life kicks in which is when they start to forget the spiritual connection they were born with. When people totally oppose this concept, and do not believe in the possibility of the spirit dimension, it is because their mind has totally accepted the rigid scientific explanations of things. If you have spent your life being told or believing something does not exist and that being psychic is impossible, to even investigate such a possibility is abhorrent to them. If they do not believe it then it cannot be true. Sometimes an event will happen to these people that will make them question what they have been told and shake the very foundations of their beliefs, however others would not believe it if Jesus himself materialised right before their eyes, as their mind just cannot cope with the concept. Everyone is on their own journey and path, so we must not judge each other just because we are at different levels on our soul's progression.

*~It's not the number of years we live that is important, but
the living we do in those years~*

WE START TO WAKE UP

Most of you are reading this right now because you have started to question your life in some way, or you feel that there must be more to life than what you have been led to believe, or perhaps you have questions that religion or science cannot provide the answers for. You may have had a traumatic experience or a near death experience which has prompted you to seek more answers to fill that gap inside yourself.

We are all energy in motion, with every living species on this planet being a crucial and integral part of the whole which keeps our planet alive. All animals and nature are just as important to keep the eco-system alive as we humans are. As I said earlier, if there were suddenly no animals or plants upon our planet it would not be long before there were no people either. Yet Man, in his greed and unending quest for control, power and money, is destroying the foundations that keep us all alive and the Earth providing for its inhabitants. Are humans so blind and naive to think that they are more important than the trees of the rainforests, or the wildlife on the plains of Africa?

They are not, for one cannot coexist without the other, but because humans have the most intelligent brain they believe themselves superior. Instead of using that immense intelligence to understand the important link that joins us all and to preserve it at all costs, they use it for material gain. If humans do not stop this systematic destruction of our planet, it does not take a rocket scientist to conclude that eventually our planet will be unable to replenish itself and sustain us and that we will cease to exist.

The rainforests are crucial to our ozone layer as they are the main provider of oxygen and protection to our Earth from gases and debris from space that could affect our world greatly if they were to get through. The 'Greenhouse Gases Effect' is a real one, not just a collection of mad scientist theories trying to scare everyone. Think about all the chemical waste that pours into our atmosphere from around the world every single day from global industry, the huge chimneys that throw out thick, choking smoke and smog into the air, day in day out, week in week out, year in year out. Where do you think it goes? Why do you think the people of China walk round with masks over their faces? Do you think for one moment that is healthy? One day there will be nowhere left for it all to go, apart from directly into our lungs and then we are all doomed to a slow suffocating death. Is the newest mobile phone, or the most sophisticated car worth what it is costing us? This horrific scenario is solely driven by Man's desire for money and power, but ultimately, it will be his downfall.

The human race, in its determination to make money and acquire status, is forgetting what the most important things in life are. The worst thing about this is that it is done in the name of progress under the guise of supposedly making our lives easier. Even though we are made to believe that we need all these things and, of course, come to rely on our gadgets and appliances, we really do not need them at all. The very things that have been invented for our pleasure and to make our existence more comfortable are in fact the things that will cause not only our own extinction, but that of the Earth and every living species on it. We must stop now, and find alternative methods that are not as harmful to our planet, but because there is currently less profit to be made in the 'Greener' approach, new ideas such as cars that are powered by splitting water molecules are dismissed as pseudoscience by the oil companies who would stand to lose a great deal if such technology was not suppressed.

The other thing that must stop is the poaching of animals because of its enormous environmental and karmic effects. All insects and animals have their designated place in the ecosystem, and the extinction of any one of them always has repercussions in the order of the Earth's survival and progression cycle. Let me give you an example: if all the snakes on the Earth ceased to exist then in a very short period the world would be overrun with rats and rodents. The rats would then cause disease amongst humans, and then we would have an army of diseases that we would have to try and find cures for, and millions of people would die. It would be the Black Death all over again, yet with far greater reach, as now we travel between the countries of the world with relative ease, so the spread of a global plague or epidemic would happen very quickly.

There is also a far greater number of people inhabiting the Earth now compared to the last time the Black Death struck, so the casualty list would be far higher. The virulent and terrifying Ebola disease making its presence known now is another global disaster waiting to happen unless it is contained soon by the governments responsible for it. Again, because of 'progress' and the ease with which travel between the continents is possible, Ebola could potentially kill as many as the great plagues of the past through its devastatingly efficient and catastrophic spread.

One of the biggest problems with animal poachers is the vicious circle of circumstances which they inhabit, and the law of cause and effect for their illegal trade. The poachers themselves are at the bottom of the food chain, so to speak, because they are paid to poach to feed and provide for their families. It is the organisers of the poaching business who are the profiteers. Poachers are normally very poor and killing elephants and rhino for their ivory and medicinal uses provides a more immediate income for them to feed their own children than any other opportunities they may have.

The only way to stop this senseless and often inhumane slaughter is to extinguish the demand. People who purchase goods made from ivory, or chimpanzee hand ashtrays, must be made to realise that they are responsible for the imminent extinction of elephants, rhino and tigers within our lifetime. If these people continue to value material trinkets that are bought merely in the interests of material possession and gain, without any thought to the devastating consequences their actions have on the animals, and therefore eventually on us, they need to be made aware that their actions are at the root of a catastrophic chain of events that is already having a major impact on the Earth's entire ecological system. Human beings need to wake up *now*, before it is too late.

People are so busy going about their daily lives and are so wrapped up in their own personal dramas, that they forget about the outside world. We are only a planet and as such we have as much significance as ants in comparison to the vastness of the Universe. We could be struck anytime by a meteor or be affected by a solar flare which could wipe out our electricity. If an event like this happened, how would people cope? We have become so dependent on technology and science that people are losing their natural survival skills and rely on the touch of a button or the flick of a switch to do everything for them. Again, this must change as it could be the cause of our own future annihilation. If our planet suffered a catastrophic event and all electricity vanished, which would affect sewerage and drinking water, cooking appliances, banks, computers, transport and almost every aspect of our modern lives, how many people would needlessly die because they cannot cook on a camp fire, or do not know how to purify rainwater? It makes you think, doesn't it?

It is time to realise how important all these things are, and to start working together to preserve our threatened animal species, to preserve our rainforests that oxygenate the planet and our natural habitats for animals and tribes-people, and to learn the natural survival skills our forefathers knew just in case we ever need them. The Earth has always undergone periods of change, such as the numerous Ice Ages and natural disasters, like earthquakes and tsunamis, but to think that just because we are so technically advanced that these things can not affect us, is very naive indeed. If Earth were to be hit by a solar flare, for example, it would happen regardless of what scientific advancement level we have on the Earth plane. The newest mobile phone or fastest internet connection will not help you in any way, but being able to feed yourself, find water and create shelter from the land, well, that just might.

~True love of Self is the greatest love of all. Master this and you master life~

THE CIRCLE OF LIFE

As I have just described, for far too long humanity has been taking more from this planet than it needs and not putting enough back to keep it replenished. Nothing shows this better than the James Cameron fantastic film 'Avatar'. This film shows how we should be treating our planet and the life-forms upon it, that everything is living energy and communicates and coexists together.

So, what happens when our life energy has gone out? People use the term 'Die', but because our soul and consciousness are energy they cannot cease to exist, it is only the physical vehicle which no longer functions, and even that is designed to decompose and be absorbed by the earth. Coffins are a relatively new concept as in ages past bodies were not placed in wooden boxes. The moment our spirit separates from our physical body is the time of our 'Death' as we understand it. Our spirit is connected to our physical body by an ethereal silver thread which has been there since our spirit entered the embryo in the womb; this is our link to the spirit dimension. Many people who have 'Died' and been revived, or had near death experiences, often recall seeing themselves from outside their body, looking down on themselves and can give highly detailed descriptions of others in the room, conversations and the procedures medical staff have attempted to bring them back.

It is well known that many people have described a 'White Light' or 'Tunnel', while others see loved ones who have already passed over or Angels, and some can recall conversations with these visions telling them it is not their time and to 'Go Back'.

For all the sceptics out there, I say how can millions of people that this has happened to, myself included, be wrong. At the time of death, you will be outside your body viewing yourself. Your spirit will rise, and the silver ethereal cord will become fully stretched and the moment when that cord snaps is when medics will declare your physical body is dead. In the case of 'near deaths' your cord does not snap, but your spirit leaves your body while it decides if it is leaving permanently or coming back, and yes, you do get a choice. So, all those people who are reading this who have had near death experiences, or survived major illness or accidents, will probably understand this more than those who have not.

During our lifetimes on the Earth plane, there are five potential exit points when we can decide whether to go back to Spirit World or remain here. In much the same way as people say that a cat has nine lives, we theoretically have five. Some people will use up their entire quota of exit points until they finally reach their last, whereas others will perish physically on their first or second. An exit point is a situation that potentially could end your life, such as an accident or illness. When someone has had a near death experience they have chosen to survive that exit point and remember it consciously once they have recovered.

For any Top Gear / Grand Tour fans reading this book, you may remember when television presenter Richard Hammond crashed the dragster car he was testing in September 2006. After reaching speeds of more than 300 miles per hour, the car's front right wheel failed, causing the vehicle to spin off the track and roll several times at 200 miles an hour. Richard sustained very serious injuries which left him critically ill and lying in a coma for two weeks. This is a classic example of an exit point, where he really should have died because of his life-threatening injuries, but on the subconscious level that links him to Spirit World, Richard fought to survive. His soul chose not to exit at that point. Richard must really like his exit points as in 2017 he crashed a million-pound super-car while making the second series of 'The Grand Tour' for Amazon, again he was in a life-threatening situation, and again he survived and thankfully gets to enjoy his life and family once more.

Spirit informs me that when your pre-arranged time for your physical body to die arrives, there is no way to avoid it. If it is not your allotted time to die and you find yourself in a life-threatening situation, either through bad decisions or just by being in the wrong place at the wrong time, then this is where your exit points come into play. If you smoke, drink heavily or poison your body with drugs, then you can also go to Spirit before your pre-arranged time which would be a direct result of your own actions.

When you return to Spirit World before your time, the Karmic rules that govern suicide will apply to your situation too, because you have not learned all the lessons you were here to experience. Therefore, so many souls come back again and again, because they have not fulfilled their destiny while they are here and go back to Spirit World before they should. People often return to Spirit World during one of their exit points because life on the physical plane can be very hard and contains much suffering. Sometimes, when a person is presented with a potential exit point, they take it rather than continuing to fight and struggle on Earth. They take the lessons they have learned so far but will come back if their full Karma was not fulfilled, or they may have an exit point which is their pre-arranged time for their physical death on the Earth plane and therefore will use it for that purpose.

I myself have had three potential exit points during my physical lifetime so far. When I was born, nearly six weeks premature, my left lung collapsed, and I nearly died. The hospital said I had only a 50/50 chance of survival as I weighed just over 4lbs and was in an incubator for weeks. That could have been my first exit point in just the first few days of my life, but I chose to live, even though I would have known on a spiritual level that my life would be very hard. Having chosen to survive my very early infancy, when I was three years old our house caught fire and if my mum had been overcome with the fumes before she had chance to get my brother and I out, then that would have been another potential exit. As it was, it was a very close shave, and I believe that a higher force intervened on that occasion to make sure that we all survived.

Twelve years later, aged fifteen, I was involved in a car crash where our car went underneath a heavy goods vehicle. I walked away from that accident without even a scratch and saved our little dog's life, who had been sitting on the back shelf of the car. As we impacted she sailed through the air and would have gone through the windscreen if I had not caught her! Then, in 2005, having nearly died after contracting meningitis and encephalitis, and having my near-death experience, I chose to survive yet again. I am probably running out of exit points now, so I will be extremely careful in the future!

Not surprisingly, if you are a person who dices with death for a living or does extreme, dangerous activities because you are an adrenaline junkie, then the likelihood of your physical life terminating early is extremely high. An example of this is the physical death of someone whom I greatly admired, enjoyed watching on television, a man who was an amazing wildlife conservationist and human being: Steve Irwin.

Also, known as 'The Crocodile Hunter', Steve grew up in Australia handling venomous snakes and crocodiles for most of his life and had faced several possible exit points in his life until he reached his fifth and final while snorkelling off the coast of Queensland. During filming for his television show, in September 2006, he encountered a stingray who reacted as though Steve was an attacking shark. The stingray's tail thrashed out wildly and managed to pierce Steve's body in hundreds of places, but most significantly, the ray's tail barb punctured his heart and he was pronounced dead at the scene, aged only 44 years old. For anyone like me, who loved watching Steve and could clearly see his profound love for all animals, I don't think we ever dreamt he would die because of a stingray barb, as we all thought he would be eaten by a crocodile in the end! But it seems that Steve's life purpose was to show us viewers, safe in our comfortable armchairs at home, all about the wonders of the animal kingdom and continually put himself in danger for his and our benefit. Steve's children Bindi and Robert, carry on his work and no doubt feels his spirit with them.

As mentioned earlier, if you are in between states, where your soul has left the body for some reason, you can make the decision to stay there at that point or to come back and live on the Earth plane for a while longer. Although this is a fictional example, a good analogy for this concept can be found in the film Harry Potter, Deathly Hallows Part 2. In the scene where Voldemort 'kills' Harry in the forest and he goes to Kings Cross station where he meets the 'dead' Dumbledore it illustrates this very accurately. In that scene Dumbledore says Harry can go back, and Harry asks what will happen if he stays, to be told a train would come that would 'take him on'. Harry then weighs up his options and decides to come back where he gets to live and fight another day.

~A death is not the extinguishing of a light, but the putting out of the lamp because the dawn has come~

WHAT REALLY HAPPENS WHEN WE DIE?

The definition of 'Heaven' is returning to Spirit. As I said earlier, at the time of your physical death there will be someone waiting to take you over to the world of Spirit. This is normally a loved one who has passed and has come to give you reassurance and alleviate your fears as you 'die'. If a soul is wrenched from the body very quickly, in the case of a murder or a car accident, then your guardian angel or another angel would be there to help with the transition. It can be a very complex web of factors and events involved, but not all deaths are pre-planned or prepared for, especially in the case of where the death is unexpected and swift, for instance if a person were to take their own life, that is a choice made in the spur of the moment of severe depression, and not pre-destined. If an individual does take their own life they are not punished in any way as stated in religious books – this is an absolute lie and nonsense. Spirit is frustrated by the falsehoods people have invented to create such fears to control Man, but I will discuss this more fully later.

Your family member or angel will guide you as your soul disconnects from your physical body and they will be by your side as you cross over into Spirit World. If you wish to see other members of your family, they will be there to greet you once you have arrived. There are many different levels in Spirit World and where your soul is sent to will depend on how far advanced your soul is. If a person has been very sick for a long time whilst on the Earth plane their soul will be tired, and they go to 'Spirit Hospital' where they are nurtured back to wholeness again.

You can choose whatever you want to do whilst in the Spirit dimension. When you first arrive, the guardian assigned to you at your birth is there to greet you, and show you whether your life lessons were fulfilled, or if they were not. If not, your guardian and other teachers will try to make you realise where you went wrong and the reasons behind this. You are made to feel every hurt you may have caused others by your actions, deeds or behaviour while in your last physical manifestation. When you are in Spirit you see everything with absolute clarity and truth as you are not restricted by human emotion.

Here on Earth, in our physical bodies, our thoughts and decisions are based on what we feel about them which often misleads us. Once we are in the world of Spirit, our judgement is no longer clouded by negative emotions such as envy, hate or fear, all of which are inventions of our ego whilst in the physical state. Some people are surprised when they return to Spirit World as they begin to understand the 'True' meaning of life, and I have many clients whom I have given guidance to, when their loved one has come through and apologised for all the wrongs they have done, because at last they can see them clearly.

As you learn from these guardians you will start to progress through the different levels of Spirit. You may choose to stay in Spirit and guide others or you may choose to return to the Earth plane once more. If you have gone to Spirit earlier than you should have, as in the case of suicides for example, and you have not fulfilled what you were supposed to learn, then you will be reincarnated to do it all again. Many choose to come back to progress their soul as much as possible, and the quickest way to do that is on Earth, as it is the most physical of experiences. Earth is the toughest school by far and therefore is the quickest way to progress your soul, even though it can take many lifetimes.

There is only one energy that exists in Spirit and that is Love, for it is the only one true emotion. On the Earth plane, however, it becomes distorted and overshadowed by many other negative emotions as we live our life. The minute we pass over into Spirit all physical and bodily ills we may have had no longer exist. There is no such thing as pain and suffering in Spirit because pain is a purely physical world experience. If we could remember physically what being in Spirit feels like, when we are on the Earth plane, we would not want to be here. Such is the magnificence of the Spirit dimension.

When we pass into Spirit, we are shown the bad deeds we have done on Earth. Some souls will not accept responsibility for their actions, so will remain upon the first level. Although there is no such thing as Hell, souls who remain on the first level will not experience the pure love and joy of Spirit's higher levels. Their guides and masters will keep trying to show them the error of their ways with love, but if they refuse to acknowledge the lessons they are being taught, they will stay on this basic level, which could be classed as a type of hell, but not the same one as described in religious books. You must atone for the bad things which you have done on Earth, but if you learn your lessons from these you will progress onward to the next levels.

In the case of what we would term 'Evil' people, those who commit horrific crimes seemingly without remorse or conscience, usually fear bodily death more than most people. When the time of physical death approaches, their soul knows what is coming and when the ethereal thread is broken they do not go with their guides towards the light but choose to be reincarnated again immediately. These souls can go through this process again and again, but eventually they will no longer want to come back and be evil again, and finally will choose to face up to what they have done and the lessons they have learnt from them.

We could call this state 'Purgatory', because these souls are trapped in a cycle of negativity by their own fears. Even though there is no 'Hell', with a horned Devil and lots of fire, these continuous negative incarnations could be considered a form of hell for your soul. It is also possible that those who have done bad things will remain Earthbound after physical death, but without reincarnating into a physical body, especially if they fear atonement for their actions. This gives rise to reports of evil spirits, 'Poltergeist' and other mischievous or negative entities.

~Those whom we love never truly leave us~

DO GHOSTS AND SPIRITS EXIST?

First, let me explain the difference between a 'Ghost' and a 'Spirit'. A ghost is a memory imprint of a person in time, an apparition of a person, but one that is very transparent; in fact, you can literally see through them. A ghost cannot communicate with you either verbally or through thought as they are an imprint of a departed soul. For example, millions of people have reported seeing figures in the night on lonely stretches of roads. These types of sightings occur because a person may have died on that particular stretch of road and on the anniversary of their death others can see their outline. What you are actually seeing is an imprint of the memory of that person. Ghosts cannot hurt you in any way, shape or form and they are not confined to the Earth plane.

A spirit, on the other hand, is a living energy. If you ever see a spirit it is much more solid, and you will also experience a feeling of intense cold wherever the spirit is. A spiritual entity can communicate with you verbally or telepathically and is able to manifest its energy to move objects, interfere with electrical equipment, and if they are mischievous, can cause problems for the living. Most spiritual sightings are of loved ones and pets who have passed, or of spirit guides and angels. Most are just signs that our loved ones in Spirit are safe and well, and that they are watching over us. They will send us feathers, coins, butterflies, birds and all manner of signs to try to communicate with us on some level. Some people can see physical manifestations, but this is rare as it takes a huge amount of energy for spirits to physically manifest on the Earth plane.

So, how does all this happen? Remember that when the ethereal cord snaps, you have the chance to go with your loved one or Guide to the Light, or what some would term 'Heaven'. Sometimes, however, certain souls do not want to cross over. When you die physically, there is a limited amount of time to pass over into the light when the portal to Spirit World opens to allow your passage. Some choose to stay and can 'lose their slot', as it were, remaining Earthbound.

Some souls want to remain Earthbound, so they can be close to their loved ones, watching over them while they go through the grieving process, but once the spirit of the deceased is satisfied their loved ones will be fine, they then pass over fully into the Spirit World. Other souls who are fearful to pass because of their actions whilst alive, remain Earthbound by choice. The Spirit World guardians will continue to encourage them to pass over, but free will exists after physical death, just as it does while you live in the physical world. Eventually, if these reluctant souls continue to refuse, the door to Spirit World will close, and that soul will become trapped here on the Earth plane, causing what are commonly known as 'Hauntings'.

A trapped spirit requires a medium to work with the angels to send them over, and normally only becomes apparent when it starts to make a nuisance of itself, interfering or scaring the living. Even though you have free will as a spirit if you are behaving mischievously then a medium, combined with the angels in Spirit World, can force the trapped soul to pass over. Other spirits can travel in and out of the Earth plane once they have progressed to that level, and this is when we find people who say they get a whiff of someone's cigarette smoke, or the scent of a familiar perfume, which they associate with their departed loved one.

There are 'Good' and 'Bad' spirits, where there is light there is also dark, as this world could not exist without opposites. People who use Ouija boards are playing with potential fire. You should never use an object to try and conjure spirits as you have no idea what you are doing, or the type of energy you are attracting. Those who practice Satanic worship, black magic, witchcraft and other similar practices, are attracting the negative type of spirits which can have devastating consequences on a person's life.

Years ago, when I first discovered my gift of spirit communication, I wanted to help the world, and was very inexperienced and naïve. In those days I used to go out to people's houses to do 'Readings'. As I pulled up outside one house on a summer evening, my stomach was in knots and my whole system was screaming for me not to go in. I thought I was being stupid, but I had a bad feeling which was very pressing and very real. But being the stubborn person, I am, I ignored my gut instinct and Spirit's warnings not to enter, and in I went.

As soon as I entered the house my hackles went up, and I felt very uncomfortable. I sat down in the lounge with my client, a single man, alone in the house. As we started talking I knew something was very wrong. My spirit Guides and Gatekeeper, (most mediums have a Gatekeeper, who stops negative spirit energy attempting to reach them) wrapped themselves so close around me that they were like a second skin. Then I felt and saw in my mind's eye, blood and pure evil like I had never felt in my life before. As I was talking to the man, I asked what on earth had gone on, as I described what I could 'See' and at the same time I was telepathically communicating with them, telling them they could not touch me as I was too well protected.

The client told me that he had done a Ouija board session recently, and he could feel these evil spirits too. He was now hearing voices in his head telling him to kill his wife! At that moment my Guide was shouting at me inside my head telling me to "Get out NOW!" I stood up and ran as fast as I could out of the front door. I've already mentioned people who go back to Spirit before their time because they ignore their 'gut'. Well, I was very nearly one of them. I learnt two valuable lessons that night, the main one being how dangerous meddling with Ouija boards and other conjuring methods can be. A genuine medium has no need of these things to communicate with Spirit. I passed this man on to a 'rescue medium' who managed to help him. The second lesson was to always listen to Spirit and to my gut instinct.

~You do not always have to see to believe~

WHO CAN COMMUNICATE WITH SPIRIT?

The answer to this question you may not believe, as the answer is: Everyone! Every living human being on this planet could communicate with Spirit world if they so choose. People have been communicating with Spirit since time began, and religious scriptures that say it is 'Devil's Work' are man-made, because if individuals chose to connect to their Higher Self, as we all can, there would be no need for religion at all, because the answers would be provided directly from 'Source'. It was because of religion's need to create fear to control Man that it declared that the ability to communicate with Spirit was something bad.

What you must understand completely is that we are all energy, and by the very nature of this we all are permanently connected to Source (Spirit World). Before we reincarnate into another physical body, whilst in Spirit World we are energy, when our soul incarnates in to a new physical body here on the Earth plane we are still energy, and when our physical body dies we become energy once more as we return to 'Heaven'. Some people can see the energy field which surrounds every living thing on the planet; this is what is called your 'Aura'. This is not a fanciful thing, this is an actual physical thing you can see, which all the sceptics out there try to dismiss, and scientists are still trying to figure out.

Because you are energy you simply cannot die. Your physical body will cease to exist of course, however your energy is eternal. You are an energy being in a physical body, with the ethereal part of you always connected to its origins in the Spirit World, and to every other living thing on the Earth, because they are energy as well. You may have heard the expression 'Energy in Motion', which is exactly what we all are and as such we are part of, and continually connected to, the whole. Therefore, every single person here on Earth, if they re-learned how to connect to 'Spirit World', could do so because they were never really disconnected in the first place. They have merely forgotten that they are energy and that they can tap in whenever they should choose to.

The reason genuine psychics or mediums can communicate with Spirit World is because they have never lost their connection to Source. As I said in the first chapters, all children are still connected to Spirit until they are about eight or nine years old, and that is why children speak about their invisible friends, or experience remembering past lives freely, because life has not infringed on them yet and shown them that the ability to do this is strange or wrong. When children are continually told that they are liars, or that they should not talk about these things because it is a sign of the Devil they begin to believe that it is wrong, soon learning to disconnect and shut it out, because when we are children our parents must be right as they are our leaders, and we must be wrong.

Most children want to be loved and to please their parents, so they naturally immerse themselves in their family's life and adhere to the teachings of adults and religious teachers, so that the beliefs of the material world, rather than the spiritual dimension, becomes their truth. In the case of mediums, this differs.

It often seems that the vast majority of genuine mediums have had very challenging experiences throughout their lives, normally starting in childhood. The difference with mediums is that even though they are told that their psychic gift is wrong, they instinctively know that they are right, and will keep their abilities a secret, conforming to adult wishes, yet know in their heart that there is more to what they are being told. They will continue to have paranormal experiences or to 'See' or 'Hear' Spirit no matter how much they try to shut it out. They just 'Know' things about people but have no idea *how* they know these things. The fact is they just do, and this can be frightening and confusing to a child, as I know from personal experience. From what Spirit has told me, even though every single person can communicate with Spirit World, there are varying degrees of connection and ability. The way in which they explain it is; "Everybody can kick a football, but we are not all David Beckham."

Those psychics or mediums who have a very strong connection and go on to help others with their gift have not always done so willingly. Normally some major trauma or event will happen in their adulthood which then brings their connection to Spirit flooding in until they can no longer dismiss or ignore it. In my case, even though I had always had a 'knowing' about things, I did not realise what it was. In 2005 I contracted meningitis and encephalitis and nearly died. It was then that my awareness came in like a tidal wave. I started hearing voices in my head and seriously thought that the illness had affected my brain and I was going mad! I had been to see a couple of mediums in the past and, to be honest, thought it was a complete load of rubbish, as nothing I had ever been told had come true.

Then, when all this started happening I came across Mary Holt, a medium in Leigh, near where I lived. She told me I had been sick and that the voices I could hear were 'Spirit' and that the reason I had contracted meningitis was because I was on the wrong path in life and this had all happened to make me aware of what I was supposed to be doing in my life.

As you can imagine this was very difficult to accept, especially for someone who had always been very sceptical about this type of thing. Mary ran a development class that I started to attend, and as my awareness began to open, the knowledge came flowing in. During one of these sessions we were asked to pick out a spiritual destiny card from a pack, and Mary said that she knew then what my new direction would be, as I picked 'The Path of Service', which is what I have been doing ever since. I also met a wonderful healer called Ted Royle whilst attending these classes and he was my first experience of past life connections, which I will talk about in a later chapter. Ted and I are still friends to this day ten years later.

So, in my case, the link to Spirit is very strong and the messages and future predictions I receive for people that come true not only astound them but me also. There have been many people throughout history who have had an exceptional connection to Spirit: Jesus Christ was the greatest healer who has ever walked the Earth so far. Harry Edwards was also an amazing healer and Moses had an amazing link to Spirit, as did the prophet Nostradamus. There are thousands more of course, and even though the Bible states that Moses and Jesus were talking to God, they were communicating with Spirit World. As I mentioned earlier, every person is born with the ability to connect to Spirit world, and this ability is eternal and will continue to exist throughout the eons.

If people learned how to reconnect this natural born ability there would be no wars, famine, sickness, greed or hurt because all the answers to all questions would be given. Mediums would no longer be needed as everyone would already be able to relay messages to and from the world of Spirit. The answers to all questions are always within ourselves, all we must do is find the key to unlock them. I believe that in centuries to come people will learn how to do this and when they do, the world will become such a more peaceful and understanding world than it is now.

~When the game is over, the king and the pawn go back into the same box~

NO ROYAL BOX: LIFE IN SPIRIT WORLD

When we return to Spirit our status or wealth on the Earth plane is of no consequence. Whether you are royalty, or a road sweeper, we all go to the same place. There is no colour or race in Spirit, which makes understanding racism on Earth most difficult. What difference does the colour of someone's skin make? What does it matter what country they are from? What matters is what type of person someone is, if they are good and kind, if they are honest and brave - their packaging is irrelevant. No one person is superior to another because of their skin colour, or because they have more money or social standing than the next, it is what is on the inside that counts for everything. Even though I have learnt so much from what I do, and I know I should not judge others, during my incarnation as Judy on this earth plane, I really struggle with those who are racist or bigoted, and with paedophiles or people who hurt children. I know as long as I live in this lifetime I will never understand it.

The saying 'There are no pockets in shrouds' is so true. It matters not what material possessions you have on the Earth plane, you cannot take it with you. The richest man on the earth will go to *exactly* the same place as the poorest when they pass over, and there is no class or gender distinction, or religious divide. There are no separate sections for people of different religions contrary to popular belief. Once they arrive in Spirit World, those who have fought for or died in the name of religion soon realise that the only place it mattered was on the Earth plane, but unfortunately there are only a few who understand this fact before they pass over.

If the people on Earth who cause war or conflicts because of religion, dictatorship, or greed could get a glimpse of what happens when we go back home to Spirit, they would stop what they are doing and try to find a more peaceful way. But again, it is all part of the greater plan and individual life lessons on the Earth plane. It is just very hard for those of us who have woken up to witness the hardship and barbarity of the world when it all means nothing when you are 'dead'.

There are those who will always revolt against what is wrong with the world and will leave a legacy of greater awareness behind them, and positive change will follow in their wake. If their actions are carried out for the good and love of the world then this is to be commended, but if their actions are born out of hatred and destruction then this is to be condemned. One of the greatest men who 'rose up' against what is wrong in the world in my lifetime was Nelson Mandela. One of the men who ruled by destruction and hatred was Adolf Hitler.

Once you have passed over into Spirit World, and been inducted back to the spiritual form, and have understood your life lessons, or what you did or did not learn while you were in physical form, you can then choose what you do next. What you must understand is, that there is no concept of time as we understand it in a physical, earthly sense in Spirit, and a year can seem like a minute. There is no urgency to complete things, unlike here on Earth, because your spiritual life and soul are eternal. Spirit World is incomprehensible to us in human existence, so I will try and describe it in a human context as best I can.

Imagine or visualise a field of poppies and focus on the vibrant red of the poppies set against the backdrop of the green meadow. Now turn those colours that you can see in your mind's eye up a million times! Every colour is so sharp, is in brilliant contrast and is so outstandingly beautiful, that we can barely even imagine it. There is a feeling of utmost peace and tranquillity, like a still lake set against the towering mountains in the middle of nowhere, in a place where mankind has never reached and therefore has never spoilt. You are forever wrapped in love and peace which you wear as a constant companion in Spirit World, all you do is simply 'Be'. You become at one with everything and every other soul around you, choosing to do whatever it is you choose to do when you have returned home.

Souls do not just float around all day doing nothing on fluffy clouds because every soul has a purpose or role to fulfil, depending on the spiritual level they have reached. For instance, I know my own mother who passed over in 2010, is there to greet and to help souls who have been abused and battered women on the Earth plane, and souls who come over because of being murdered by their spouse whilst in physical form. She chose this because she herself was battered and abused all her physical life as my mum, at first by her stepmother and then by my father, so the experience and knowledge gained during her incarnation allows her to help other souls. I am pleased to say my Mum did not die as a result of domestic abuse; she divorced him thirty years before her physical death here. Sadly, not all women are that fortunate.

In Spirit World there are schools and 'Halls of Learning' dedicated to teaching souls whatever they need to learn on their journey of progression. Some of these Halls of Learning are where souls are made aware of what they need to experience during their next incarnation on Earth, or to which ever dimension they are journeying to next. When babies pass over before birth, in the case of terminations or miscarriages, they go to a special place in Spirit where they are nurtured by 'Angel Mothers'. These Angel Mothers are souls who have passed and chosen to fulfil this role. The spiritual beings overseeing all of this are actual Angels, spiritual beings who have never chosen to incarnate, but remain in Heaven connected to the God Source, where they dedicate their existence to teaching and the spiritual evolution of all other beings.

The baby souls are loved and cared for until they grow into small children, where they then advance to the 'Spirit Nursery'. Even if you have lost a baby here on the Earth plane before it was born, you will be reunited with it once you return to Spirit yourself. Sometimes the part of the soul which made up that embryo will choose to come back again to Earth as another child you may have years later. It all depends on what stage an embryo is at before it is lost, as a soul does not always enter the body of a baby in the womb until it is at a certain development stage. If the soul has already entered the baby, it may choose to come back, or if the pregnancy has ended in the early stages, yet if a soul has already chosen to be born to you then it will come back in a later pregnancy.

In the case of infants and children who have been physically born pass over to Spirit, the physical age of the child dictates where it will go. Young infants and toddlers will go to another Spirit Nursery where souls who were related to them on Earth will dedicate themselves to looking over the child's soul until such a time as the child has grown and advanced in the world of Spirit to higher levels or has decided to return to the Earth plane or another dimension for an incarnation once more. Older children are normally met by a family member when they pass over. During their adjustment, the family member will love and guide them, and the child will attend a school of learning which develops and enhances their spiritual evolution.

If a child's life has been ended by someone before the child was supposed to return home, then a part of that soul will return to Earth to fulfil its 'Blueprint' and destiny. If you have lost a child you will be reunited with the part of the soul that was your child, and you will recognise each other immediately, no matter how many Earth years have passed in the meantime. Children who have passed can choose to grow or they can remain at a certain age: it is the free will of that individual soul, but even if the child has chosen to become an adult in the world of Spirit, you will know that this is your lost child and you will be together at the time of your own passing. The only time this differs is if you have committed suicide, and you may not be reunited with your child until you have gone through a recovery process in Spirit World yourself.

Teenagers and young adults who take their own life are not punished as many religions have proclaimed. They are lovingly educated by their own guides and angels on the reasons they took that action while here. Again, the majority of those who have taken their own life return to Spirit prematurely and therefore need to come back to learn their unfinished lessons and to fulfil their Karma. Please do not think as you are reading this that this is a hardship for them, because once you return home to Spirit, your soul remembers everything about being in Heaven before. It is only the physical body and mind that become distorted by the experiences in the physical realm, so once you are free of your physical body, the reasons you were here in the first place become crystal clear again.

Earth is the toughest but most effective school for the evolution of your soul. If you are already highly evolved, you may choose to come back in a non-human form, or to have that experience in a completely different dimension. On the other hand, if you have fulfilled your Karma, you may decide to remain in Heaven to teach and help evolve souls there. Even when you have learnt everything in your incarnations, some souls still decide to return to the Earth voluntarily to help others here in the physical world. Some souls enjoy having physical experiences again and again, even if they are tough.

Just to clarify a couple of points about angels: Several angels have come to Earth for a physical existence, one of them being the Archangel Metatron. Generally, however, an angel does not incarnate as a soul on the Earth plane as they are pure spiritual beings who are directly connected to the collective consciousness that we call 'God'. I will talk about this in the chapter on Religion.

So, once you are back in Spirit and had further lessons you then decide it is time to come back. The total understanding of this concept only becomes clear when we have returned to Spirit. An individual soul, which is a separate entity to a person, can be made up of hundreds of parts. A soul is made up of every incarnation it has ever had, so if it has had five incarnations, it is made up of five parts; if it has had a thousand incarnations, it is made up of those. When a soul decides it wants to have another experience on Earth, or whatever dimension it wants to sample next, it will first have that 'Thought'. It then seeks the counsel of more experienced souls and if they agree that this would be a progression for the soul, the incarnation is permitted. The soul then creates another part for itself and chooses what lessons it wants to learn and which parentage it should be born to in order to facilitate these lessons.

The new part of the soul enters the body of the baby during the later stages of pregnancy, or at the time of birth. A soul is always in place by the time of physical birth as a human being, and this is where it becomes really mind-blowing! A soul can decide it wants to experience more than one existence at the same time, in different physical bodies, and therefore it will create more than one new part for itself. Indeed, it can create multiple parts if it chooses and it has been agreed that this will benefit the soul. This is where twins or multiple births arise. The soul has decided it wants to be able to have multiple experiences at the same time in different physical bodies yet at the same time remain part of the whole. Let's take twins for example: some twins may look identical, yet their life experiences and personalities will be totally separate from each other, even though their reflection in the mirror is identical.

Twins usually embody the concept of light and shade, often possessing totally opposing personalities, which allows the main soul to experience opposite experiences concurrently during the same lifetime. This accelerates their spiritual progression, rather than having to come back in two separate lifetimes to achieve what they can in just one lifetime. A soul who wants this multiple experience at the same time can also choose completely different bodies, with separate sets of parents, and at different intervals of time. They can also decide if they want any of these different physical bodies to cross paths with the other one during their years on Earth.

You have probably heard the term 'Soulmate' which does not always denote a romantic connection. If you meet someone whom you deem to be your soulmate, this could be due to having come in to contact with an individual who was created by the same soul that created you, or because you have had other incarnations with that soul in a past life and that is why you feel such a strong connection. An example of soulmates in existence right now who people reading this now may know, are Prince Charles and Camilla, another is the world famous ice-skating partnership of Jayne Torvill and Christopher Dean. In the first example, no matter whether you were a die-hard Princess Diana fan or not, there can be no dispute that Charles and Camilla were always destined to find each other, weathering all the media intrusion into their lives, surviving the whole messy Charles and Diana divorce, to finally be with each other. They were destined to find each other before they were born. They may not even be consciously aware of it, but their connection to each other is so strong and so effortless that they are just meant to be.

Although soulmates are not always romantically tied, if you *do* have a romantic connection to someone who is your soulmate then you are in a minority and that link between you is one of the most fulfilling on Earth. If you are destined to be with someone, then you will find them eventually, although you can be happily married to someone who is not your soulmate. In each relationship you will often find that you love in a different way and the soulmate connection defies space and time. If you do marry your soulmate, then you will remain inseparable and only death with divide you and even then, you will be reunited again in Spirit World.

Then there are the stories of twins who have been separated at birth yet find each other in a world full of seven billion people, fall in love and get married without knowing they are related to each other, until a blood test or a similar type of event reveals this connection further down the line. How did they gravitate towards each other? What pulled them together? It is their 'Soul Connection'.

The other thing I want to share with you about twins, or those from multiple births, is their psychic link to each other. It is a 'soul link' but many people would also call this psychic, and I had personal experience of this before I ever realised that I was a medium. I was permanently fostered from the age of twelve and when I was fourteen my foster-mum's niece had twin girls. Now, I have always loved children, and I adored these two girls, as well as their older sister who was three years old when they were born. They were a little premature, as twins can be, and one was born with a hole in her heart, yet the other slightly bigger twin was perfectly healthy.

The twin with the hole in her heart had to remain in hospital while the healthy twin was allowed home, and one night we had her overnight while her mum stayed with the poorly twin in the hospital. At 3a.m. she kicked off screaming at full pitch for no apparent reason, this was unusual because this twin was the more laid back one of the two. About forty minutes later she stopped abruptly and went straight back to sleep with no other problems. We found out the next day that at precisely the same time in the hospital over thirty miles away, her twin had kicked off at *exactly* the same time and stopped at the same time! The baby staying with us had picked up on her sister's distress.

Some would dismiss that as coincidence, but I know there is no such thing.

As stated earlier, your Soul is made up of every incarnation and experience you have ever had, so even if the soul has created a new part or multiple new parts so it can be reincarnated, those newly created parts are still connected to the whole soul that resides in Spirit World. Remember when we spoke about how we are all energy which is why we are eternal? And about how we are connected to spirit world always by our ethereal thread or cord? Well, this principle applies to the whole soul too. Therefore, you can remember past lives and sometimes bring negative emotions over from them, because you are always connected to the whole. The whole soul is made up out of everyone or everything you have ever been, and you can tap into this reservoir of knowledge and experience at any time.

If you have returned to this plane because of an unfulfilled lessons or karma, then you may experience similar things from a previous lifetime. You are part of and connected to what some people might call "All that is, all that was, and all that will ever be" continually during your incarnation here, or indeed any other existence you inhabit. Another important part of your human make-up is your physical matter, so although your created soul is completely its own entity, you are also constructed from DNA, genetics, cultural influences and family heritage. We are very complex and intricate beings. Your subconscious, which is linked to your soul, is where you access past life memories because all information is stored here, from this lifetime and others. You may have chosen to return to the same family that you were in before, therefore you will have a genetic link and memories as well as links of a spiritual nature. Genetic illnesses can be passed through our physical matter and DNA; however, we would only have reincarnated into that body if that is what we chose before we came back.

Spirit has asked me to clarify one more thing about souls once and for all. There are many spiritual people who believe that the soul splits into twelve separate parts when it leaves your body and goes back to Spirit World. Some have also been told that your soul is made up of multiple parts while it is in your physical body. This is not true. The master soul which resides in Spirit World has indeed created many living parts along its journey, however when a soul enters a new baby it is only one soul. The reason you can remember past lives when under hypnosis or indeed when people have spontaneous flashbacks of other lives, is because you are always connected to your parent soul in Spirit World. Therefore, every experience or lesson you have is transmitted back through your link to the main soul, and every experience the main soul has had is accessible to you also.

Let me try to explain this further: think of it like a computer. When you insert a memory stick, you can upload information to the hard drive where it is permanently stored, yet that same process allows you to download information stored on your hard drive back onto the memory stick. When you disconnect the memory stick from your computer the information is still stored within it. This is the best analogy that Spirit can find to illustrate this concept.

So, in some ways, the idea of 'Same Soul, Different Bodies' is correct because the main soul in Spirit World has created many soul parts to reside in different bodies. It gains all the lessons and experiences needed to progress itself, yet it creates a completely new part for itself when it wants to reincarnate into a new individual. The new part of the soul is connected always to the main, or master soul, through our ethereal cord and mind energy link. All experiences are uploaded and downloaded between them, which is how we retrieve past life experiences and memories.

When the part that has been your soul in your physical body returns to Spirit World, the reason it can go off and learn other things by itself is because it was individual in the first place. Say, for instance, that your soul passes back to Spirit World after you have taken your own life. You will not have fulfilled your lessons or Karma if you have returned too soon, so all those experiences are transmitted back to the main soul. Your individual part of the main soul which is the essence of the person you were when here, can choose to create another part for itself and come back in to another physical body to fulfil what it did not do the first-time round. So, the ethereal part of you that was 'John Smith' remains in Spirit World, and the new part you have created will come back in another physical body yet remain connected to you *and* the main soul which first created the 'John Smith' soul! That is also where past life memories are created, because if you or 'John Smith' have created another soul part to come back for lessons you did not fulfil, then your past life link could be very strong, and you could also bring negative feelings or emotions over with you in to your new incarnation. I know, it is utterly mind boggling isn't it?

I must say that before I started writing this book with Spirit, I believed it was just one soul that came back in different incarnations, and I have to say that Spirit has completely blown my belief and understanding right out of the window. I must also add that your main soul will also have had animal incarnations throughout its progression and evolution, and during past life regressions it has been known for that information to be downloaded to you from your main soul in Spirit World. The soul created at your incarnation always remains in Spirit World, which is how mediums like me can communicate with loved ones who have passed over. If we were just the same soul coming back in different bodies then the person you were on Earth would cease to exist when the physical body of that individual died, however this is not the way it is, the essence or ethereal part of you that was contained in your physical body is eternal.

~The true measure of a person is not how many times they are knocked down, but by how many times they get back up~

THE AKASHIC RECORDS & PAST LIVES

The Akashic Records are an individual record of each soul's incarnations, which resides permanently in Spirit World. Each main soul, as we determined before, creates many parts for itself to have the many experiences it needs to become whole, and the details of each incarnation is what is known as an Akashic Record. There is a monumental library in Spirit World containing these records, and the library is overseen and organised by angelic beings. Each record contains all your experiences from the past as well as lessons and karma that need to be learnt from your future incarnations. Therapists here on the Earth plane can explore these areas, both past and present, while their client is in an altered state.

If you are a therapist who uses Future Life Progression, you must be very careful to make sure your client does not see anything that is detrimental to them in the future. Any negative responses can be eliminated when dealing with past lives, however, it cannot be extinguished when projecting the future, as the lessons that are being seen will have been prearranged before that incarnation. In some cases, to see it now, could do serious emotional and mental damage to someone for the rest of their physical life here. Unless necessary, my guides tell me that progression in to future lives serves no purpose and could be quite damaging to the person. Progression to time frames in the present life can help people who are struggling with what path to take in life presently, but again, the therapist must control the session, so the client only sees what can help them, not hinder them.

When someone seeks the counsel or guidance of a medium to find out what their future holds for them, a good medium will identify what is holding them back now and guide the client to future choices and possible outcomes, yet at the same time making it very clear that a client has free will and has to make their own choices. If a client was under hypnosis and saw their own future possibilities in this life, or indeed another, depending on the state of mind of the client at the time, could make what they are seeing false, as they have created it themselves. If they glimpse bad elements of their future, then they are going to firmly believe them to be true as they have 'seen' it themselves, so you must be extremely careful when dealing with things like this. Spirit does not like the idea of future projection, unless it is undertaken by spiritually minded people and the person leading it makes certain when programming that nothing detrimental will be seen, unless it would save that person's life, or help them to make the right choices in their future.

When I was developing my connection to Spirit years ago I went to the Akashic Records during a meditation and it was a wonderful experience. My main soul has been creating parts for human experiences since 10 A.D. My guide has told me that my main soul, and the part which currently resides in my body, will create new parts that will come back a further seven times here on the Earth, which will take another 1,000 to 1,500 years to complete, depending on how long each of my soul's learning experiences are in Spirit World. By the time my incarnations here on the Earth are over I will have attained complete spiritual evolution and have prophet status in my final incarnation on the Earth plane. At that time, my physical being will be a male and the world will be at a crucial point, requiring many other prophets to help guide humanity, as well as beings from other dimensions, if the world is to survive for another billion years or so.

So now we need to ask the question: are past lives real? Past lives are very real and are stored in the main soul which resides in Spirit World always, and the reason we can access them is because we can upload and download these memories and experiences like a computer. Also, the soul that lives in your body right now as you are reading this, could be a new individual soul, or partly made up of someone you were in a past life that needed to come back and re-experience life on the Earth as it did not fulfil its original karma.

Before a person's new incarnation on Earth, the main soul wants to create a new part for itself to experience this and has to create a 'Blueprint' or 'Soul Contract' for the new part that is going to come in to the body of a human being. A blueprint, or soul contract, is the binding pact set out detailing the main lessons and any Karmic debt that the soul will be incarnated to learn this time. This is where your Earth parents are chosen, where it is arranged that certain people will cross your path in life at predestined times, if you will have any physical or mental imparity, if you will be rich or poor, what race and ethnic group you will be born in to, what country you will be born in, what gender you will be, and if you have any special gifts, for example, a genius like Einstein.

The blueprint is the 'nuts and bolts' of your existence on the Earth plane, and although all the main events that you will experience are already pre-arranged, or fated, to a certain extent, your choices here whilst incarnated in human form are crucial too, as unfortunately we cannot remember physically what these lessons are which were arranged in our blueprint. Additionally, before you are reincarnated in to a physical body you also choose at what time physically you will return to Spirit World. Your age of death is arranged before you are even incarnated, and as we have stated in previous chapters, because you cannot physically remember this, some of the choices we make, and the positions we find ourselves in through our own making or that of others, can take us back to Spirit World before our allotted time.

Many children seem to be able to remember past lives spontaneously without being under hypnosis, in fact, I had personal experience of this in my own life as well as that of my children's lives. From about the age of four or five years old, I kept seeing in my mind's eye a young girl of about nine or ten, dressed in a grey uniform holding a lantern and I just knew that her name was Emily, or Emmie, as she was known. I kept on seeing her on and off all my life up to the time of contracting meningitis in 2005 and when I started to learn about my gift of mediumship. When I had past life regression with Mary Holt, this was the first life that came up. We discovered that Emily was a serving girl in the 1800's and had died of consumption at the age of ten. We also found out during the regression sessions that most of my lives had been ended by tuberculosis (known at the time as consumption), which is a disease of the lungs.

The weird thing is that when I was born in this lifetime, I was five weeks premature and my left lung collapsed at birth and I had a 50/50 chance of survival. If I ever got a cold it always went to my chest, and I cannot be in smoky atmospheres as it can really affect me. It's as though I brought a weak lung over with me in to this incarnation! I know many of you reading this will think that it is just a coincidence, however knowing what I do now about how sometimes things can follow you from previous lifetimes I do not believe it is a coincidence as I have seen too much evidence over the years that just cannot be explained.

As a fully qualified hypnotherapist, I also conduct past life regressions for clients and have found that most phobias are created in a past life. I had a young female client that was petrified of travelling on motorways, and of the lorries that rumble along them daily. She had to use a motorway to commute to work, but every time she got in her car she would sweat and shake behind the wheel and arrive at work a complete nervous wreck.

When I am using hypnotherapy to treat a client, unlike many therapists I do not lead the client, I just ask for them to go back to the root cause of whatever is causing them a problem. This girl went back to a previous incarnation as a male lorry driver, where he had a heart attack at the wheel and had caused the death of many people, but not himself on a motorway, therefore, this is where her fear of driving on motorways and lorries had come from. A good past life regression therapist will always eliminate the negative emotions that a client has brought over, so it no longer impedes their current life. I am so honoured to be able to have helped so many people using this therapy.

During my development into spirituality I met a man called Ted Royle who is a wonderful naturally gifted healer. There was an instant connection between us which at the time I could not understand, as Ted is twenty years my senior. It was so strong, in fact, it almost felt like a love connection, that we both decided to have a regression session to see if it was past life related. Mary Holt regressed us both separately without telling the other what we had said. Ted and I both had the same past life experience, one as husband and wife and then Ted as my son. How can two people who have never met in this life before, have such a connection and experience the same two past lives under hypnosis?

I have two sons in this life, who are both spiritually connected even though the eldest one tries to deny it! Yet it is him who had extreme past life memories as a child and of course this was long before my own journey as a medium had begun. At this time, I was a travel agent, and Ryan was about four when he first started saying things about other lives. Bearing in mind the most complex thing he could watch on television was Scooby Doo and the Teletubbies, this was really quite surprising!

One day, in the living room at home, he became terribly upset for no apparent reason. When I asked him what was wrong, he said he was sad because he missed his brother John. I told him he did not have a brother at that time, but he insisted. I was curious, so I asked him to tell me what he meant. He said that he had a brother called John, and that he and John were dead in a coffin and that they had a man with a big moustache that they had to call Father. He said he and John had been killed by men with guns. If you could have seen how incredibly sad he was as he told me this, no one would have been able to say what he was saying was not true to him.

I was utterly perplexed, so I did a little research on past life memories. Then, over the next few years, he started to experience past lives in dreams. On another memorable occasion, not long after his first experience, Ryan again described the astonishingly vivid details from another past life that would have been impossible for a child so young to know anything about. He said he was surrounded by men in white cloaks holding burning crosses, and on the floor was a black man lying on a tablet of stone. I mean, how does a four-year-old know the meaning of a 'tablet' of stone? I asked him if he was one of the men in the white cloaks or the black man. He said he was the black man named Elijah, and that he had been killed.

To say this blew my mind is an understatement, but of course now I know that Spirit had gradually been preparing me for what was to come for me, but at the time I just could not comprehend it. Again, it is one of those events that many people might call coincidence, yet it could be a clear explanation of why my son cannot stand racism, the same as me.

My youngest son Alex, at the age of about four or five, spoke of hiding in long grass when men came and set fire to his wooden home, and that he had other brothers and sisters. Alex has not had the same past life memory connections as Ryan, but he is very in tune with his higher self. When clients come to see me, Alex will often receive the correct names of people connected to the client, and like me at his age he is just 'knows' things about people. He also knows all words to songs from the 80's when he hears them on the radio even though he has not heard them before, he was born in 2004! I do not encourage his connection yet, as I want him to remain a child for as long as possible and I try to keep what I do away from my sons' friends, as I do not want them to be ridiculed by those that do not believe in what I do.

I know it is very hard, if not sometimes near impossible, to understand and accept that we have chosen our life and experiences before we were even born into it, but the aim of this book is to try to help you to understand how and why you came in to existence in the first place, and to guide you towards spiritual enlightenment and awareness. When we have had very bad things happen to us along our journey in life, and when we have suffered poverty and hardship, as have I in this incarnation, it can make all this very difficult to comprehend. The fact that we have chosen it as part of our experience for the lessons we learn and for our soul's evolution and growth is quite unbelievable to many.

I have struggled greatly in this incarnation, and see the heartbreak and grief of the people that I deal with as a medium, so I constantly question the reasons and the meaning of it all. I believe Spirit chose me to write this book, to teach me as well as hopefully teaching and helping others. Through all my trauma and challenges in life I questioned the purpose of human existence and why people suffer in the way that they do, and there has been a number of times that I have despaired, telling Spirit that I will no longer work for them, as I cannot bear the cruelty and barbarity with which human beings treat each other. Yet, as they are channelling all this information through me to compose this book, I know with absolute certainty that it is the truth.

Even though the physically human part of me struggles to accept it, my higher self or my soul, knows that this is all fact, whether I or indeed anyone else embraces this knowledge and adapt our lives accordingly is a matter of choice. The facts, however, will always remain the same, and if we choose to dismiss this knowledge as complete rubbish, when our physical body no longer exists and our soul returns home to Spirit

World, then the truth will be available to us in all its divinity once more.

~If you can't change your fate, change your attitude~

LESSONS AND DESTINY

Your lessons and destiny cannot be changed from what is laid out in your blueprint. Whatever lessons you have agreed to before you come back will stay with you even if you do not fulfil them when you are supposed to in this life. Your destiny is something that has been agreed before you are incarnated on the Earth plane and will happen to you. If something is your destiny, it may not happen at the precise time it was supposed to, should your life choices have interfered with it in some way, however eventually it will. There is something that must be made crystal clear here: If something is not your destiny, no matter how many dream boards you make, no matter how much positive projection you do, it will simply not happen.

Let us take for example someone who wants to be a famous singer, if it is your destiny for this to happen, the doors of opportunity will open for you at just the right time and away you will go, but if it is not your destiny, no matter what you do and how hard you push, you will not get that right opportunity and it will not happen for you. There is a fine line here, destiny will not happen for you until it is the right time, but no matter what path you are on in life, destiny will come to find you. That does not mean if you have been trying to get noticed for years that it will not happen for you ever, it just means it may not have been your time until now. For example, the runner-up contestant of the Britain's Got Talent TV show, Susan Boyle. Susan did not fulfil her destiny until it was her time at the age of forty-six. Even though Susan came second in the final, she has gone on to have global success as a singer.

So how can we tell whether to pursue something or to give up trying? When something is your destiny, there will be a burning desire, a passion that you cannot even explain to yourself, it will be a knowing deep within you that this is what completes you. On the other hand, if you are just pursuing something because you want fame and fortune, or not for genuine reasons, if is not something you love deep in your soul, then you will not achieve it, irrelevant of how much you project it. Sometimes one's destiny descends on them unexpectedly and out of the blue, for instance if you win the lottery.

There is a true story of a woman who always used the same numbers for the lottery. Money was tight for her family, her husband had to stop work due to sickness and they had a baby to look after. This woman worked a couple of jobs to make ends meet, and one day she had to choose between nappies for her baby or putting on the lottery, naturally she chose the nappies, but her numbers came up and she lost out on 6.7 million pounds. She vowed never to do the lottery again and for four years worked her butt off providing for her family, then one night she had a dream that she won the lottery. The dream was so real that even though she had not done the lottery for those four years she felt compelled to do it. Two weeks after her dream she won 4.9 million. Coincidence? No way. She was always destined to win it, but her choices just meant it happened later than it would have done originally. Yet maybe it did happen at the right time, as after struggling for all those years since missing out on the original win, she may appreciate it more that she would have done then and learnt many life lessons along the way. When something is your destiny there is no escaping it, it will happen in your life no matter what obstacles stand in the way.

If someone had told me thirteen years ago that it was my destiny to become a well-known medium, to write this book and that I would be able to communicate with Spirit World I would have suggested a straightjacket for them! When I was a little girl, and right up to being a late teenager, when anyone asked me what I wanted to be the answer was very simple, I always wanted to be a police officer. Unfortunately, life seemed to be working against me, as I ended up on my own with a four-month-old baby around the time I wanted to join and it was not meant to be. I know now that it was not my true destiny, but in those early years I could not understand why I was unable to achieve what I wanted.

What was not clear to me at the time is that the universe had bigger plans for me, and now I have helped thousands of people whose paths I would never have crossed had I been a police officer, yet this path has been very hard, and I am a typical example of unexpected destiny. Throughout my childhood and early adulthood, I always tried to help people (which is one of the reasons I wanted to join the police force), but not for one moment did I ever envisage that it would be through my spiritual connection that I would help people. It never crossed my mind, but that is the wheels of destiny for you. I bet when Nelson Mandela was incarcerated in an awful South African prison, he never, ever dreamed that one day he would be President of the country he had fought to make free. Destiny.

Life lessons can come in various ways, often in very upsetting disguises. The things which happen to us on our journey that fill us with sadness and grief can be the biggest lessons of all, yet at the time we rarely see the reasons why a tragedy has happened. As stated before, when you agree your blueprint in Spirit World before you are incarnated into a physical body on Earth, this is when you will choose the lessons. Sometimes the lessons are not for you alone, or not for you at all, as you will also play a part in your family's lessons and destiny. Those who are born with physical or mental disabilities or impairments have chosen to experience this during their lifetime, even though we may find this extremely difficult to comprehend. The same applies to babies who are born with sickness or disease, and for children who are only here for a short time in earth years and then return to Spirit.

As humans, we usually only see what is right in front of us, many of us failing to see the bigger picture unless we are spiritually attuned, and even then, because we are living a physical existence and experience love and loss, we will still struggle with it, even though we know the reasoning behind it. If a child is sick when it is born, then only remains on Earth a short time, the lessons are mainly for that child's parents and family as part of their lessons and destiny agreed before they were incarnated. I know this is difficult to comprehend, especially for anyone reading this who has a child that has gone back to Spirit seemingly too early, but this event was already predestined.

When I was a teenager I worked voluntarily in a youth club where we looked after able-bodied and disabled children, and I particularly loved working with those who had Down's Syndrome. Children with this condition are essentially made of pure love – that is the only way I can really describe it, and they are here to teach us lessons in acceptance, and to experience their unconditional love. If they are born to the right parents, then they will get this in return for themselves which will really evolve their soul dramatically. A person with Down's Syndrome or indeed any impairment like that, can teach us so much, and that is one of the reasons they are here.

I remember when I first started doing audience demonstrations of mediumship, I was working a platform one night and I went to a woman in the audience. I was told by Spirit that there was someone connected to her who had Down's and she confirmed this, saying it was her son. She then said something which upset me so deeply at the time that it has stayed with me and will do until the day I leave this mortal coil. She asked me if he had been sent to her as a punishment! The woman was so full of bitterness and resentment that she had a son with Down's and he was such a burden that she felt he had been born as a punishment to her. I had to remain professional and explain to her why her son had been born that way and that she should realise that it was like having her own Earth angel sitting in her living room every day. This woman simply could not see the beauty of this boy and thought I was crazy for suggesting that he was here for a special reason.

I know parents of children with disabilities can find caring for them very difficult and life-consuming, but once you understand that your soul asked for this before you were incarnated, then it may help you to understand and see things differently to what you have always believed up until this point.

When children go to Spirit because they have been killed or abused in some way, as difficult as this is to believe or accept, most times it has been predestined. As a human being and a parent this is the biggest issue I struggle with the most in this physical incarnation, but sometimes there is also an element of fulfilling Karmic debt when children suffer here on the Earth. Even though certain lessons are prearranged, the way in which we learn these are taken out of our hands and into Spirit's control. When we see a child's death on the news, feeling disgust and outrage at what has happened, we rarely stop to consider that this may have already been predestined, and we just cannot comprehend it, but a soul may have chosen this demise as part of the lessons for the parents or adults connected to them.

There have been a several high-profile examples in the UK of bereaved parents who have gone on to change the laws that govern our countries and achieved great things after losing their children in horrific circumstances. Sara Payne and Doreen

Lawrence, for instance, are two of the most amazing women in my lifetime who have experienced so much heartbreak yet have chosen to do something that will benefit and help thousands in the years to come. This is where the choice again enters our lives. Bad things happen to good people every day, but it is how we deal with them that determines our existence. We can choose to become bitter, twisted and full of hate, or we can choose to turn something so negative in to a positive, to help others.

So, the answer is that our life on the Earth is made up of lessons and destiny, but it is our choices and how we respond to these that make up the person we are and the person we become. It is our choices that determine where we go from wherever we are right now in our lives. You may not achieve fame and fortune if that is not your destiny, yet if you learn to appreciate what you do have and make the choices to accept some things then you will be very rich indeed, because you will have found peace. If you can realise your connection to Source, (God), or what name you associate with the divine energy we are all a part of, then you will know that trying to live your life by yourself creates many challenges. We can choose something in our life that is wrong for us, and can waste many years trying to achieve something that just is not meant for us, but if we learn to connect to that divine energy, through prayer, or meditation, or by pure faith and trust, and follow the path that is given to us, rather than the one we think we should have, then it will lead us to where we are meant to be. There will still be events that happen to us as that is the law of nature, however, when we have that divine connection, we have much more understanding of the reasons behind the challenges we face in life, and the ability to deal with them.

~There is no need for temples, no need for complicated philosophy. Our own brain, our own heart is our temple; the philosophy is kindness~

GOD AND RELIGION

Spirit does not want to offend anyone by what is written in this chapter, however it will not deviate from the truth either. Religion has been created in order to control men through fear of retribution if your life is not lived in a certain way, obeying the rules set out by men claiming to be the mouthpiece of the Divine. The original goal of religion was very spiritual but, as we find with a game of Chinese Whispers, the true message of the Divine has been lost in translation and buried under Man's greed. Many prophets and spirit messengers have been sent to Earth from the beginning of civilisation: Moses, Lazarus, and Jesus to name but a few, yet their messages have been distorted and twisted to suit the purpose of those in positions of power at the time. Dictators always fear the ones they repress because they know that one day there will be one that will revolt against what is being taught because it is wrong, and this has been happening for centuries with different religions.

So, is there really a God? The answer to this is so simple, yet so unbelievable to many people, because the teachings of religious institutions around the world for so long have dictated that 'God' (or whatever name you choose to use, depending on your belief) is a supreme being outside of yourself who needs to be worshipped. Nothing could be further from the truth. Established religions say that God decides whether your prayers are worth his time, answers a few, but not others. These same religions say that God, (because you stole some bread to feed your starving family), decides that this is sinful and punishable by being sent to eternal hell and damnation when you die. How can a race of human beings with immense intelligence still believe such nonsense? The truth is that you are God and that God is you. You are surrounded by and connected to the eternal energy of the entire universe every single second of your life from physical birth to physical death and beyond. So, the answer to the question is: Yes, there is a God or Creator, yet without you and every other energy being it would not exist. You are connected the whole time, so God is not a supreme being outside yourself and separate to yourself. It is within you and accessible to you always, if you could learn to connect to it. If you did that, you would not need any form of religion to answer your questions as all the answers would be provided for you and to you.

It is such a simple concept, yet so hard for many people to believe, but Spirit World keeps sending its messengers to Earth, where they are killed and persecuted by dictators who want everyone to live in fear, so they will conform and line their pockets. It is a sad fact that the Catholic Church is one of the richest businesses in the world, but how can that be? Spirit tells me that the current Pope Francis has been sent to change the Catholic Church, to oust out the greed and hypocrisy within the

Vatican walls, and to bring a more spiritual essence into the religion. Spirit tells me that it matters not what one believes if it helps to give you hope and faith, and it provides sanctuary in times of need *if* the teachings are of love and helping your fellow man, not of fear and damnation. How can a member of the clergy say he is a 'Man of God' yet be a paedophile and hurt innocent children? This is not an act of God. Nuns and priests in ages past have been some of the cruellest human beings on the planet yet claimed to be acting on God's instruction. It is all so hypocritical.

A man can beat his wife and children on a Saturday whilst drunk yet go to church on Sunday and be absolved, yet if that same wife left him, because of how he treated her, this is seen as a sin!

Those who truly believe in God and are connected to the God Source energy know that this is ludicrous and is the result of brain washing through the ages. It is time that things changed once and for all for the sake of humanity, yet sadly, I cannot see this happening within my lifetime, because all those religions who make so much money from what they have led people to believe would be made to look fools, and they are not going to take very kindly to that. On the other hand, there are also amazing nuns, priests and other forms of clergy who dedicate their lives to helping others, providing comfort and help to those in need, and they do it with pure love as their highest intention. These types of people are truly connected to God Source and this must not be forgotten while some of the negatives of religion are discussed.

Any religion that uses fear, hate, violence or any negative emotion is not working in the name of God, even if they have been brainwashed in to believing that they are. When you truly believe in God or are connected to the God Source you would never use the name of God to hurt or oppress another individual or animal in any way. You would never commit murder just because someone has a different religious viewpoint or belief than you do, or torture masses of people so that they must follow your belief or inflict persecution or death just because they will not conform to your way of thinking.

Religion is the biggest cause of death. Fact. It is responsible for more deaths throughout the ages than all illnesses of the world put together. It is responsible for most wars, terrorist attacks, and human segregation than any other thing ever invented. I don't know about you, but I find that very frightening indeed, and I know that Spirit is desperate for this to change because they can see the trauma and sorrow that it has caused in the past and continues to cause now. Back at the height of the troubles in Northern Ireland, two separate beliefs caused so much death and sorrow, yet how can anyone who hurts or kills another because they do not believe the same as them, say they believe in God when one of the Ten Commandments in the Christian religion is 'Thou Shalt Not Kill'? How can anyone say that they are being true to their religion when they are clearly breaking one of their own commandments in the name of the God they are supposed to be following? It is just so senseless and hypocritical.

When you truly believe in God, you do not need to defend that belief, or to convince anyone else. When you are in tune with your Higher Self and God Source energy, it needs no explanation as you have the knowledge within yourself always. Share your knowledge with those who will listen, but not by force. There will be some who understand and others who will not, yet everyone is on their own path that was laid out before they even got here, and each soul will progress in its own time. Just understand that your soul is more evolved than someone else's, and do not judge what they believe to be wrong even though it is different to what you believe. Bless them with love and light, then move on.

In generations to come religions will change dramatically, and as we move into the next century there will be a lot more spiritual evolution where religions are concerned. There will always be those who try to force others to believe what they do, but this will be on much smaller scale than it is now. This can only be a good thing, as all this senseless killing and heartache, done in the name of something that should be beautiful and loving, must stop. Some of the teachings in the religious books such as the Bible, or the Koran, are highly spiritual and correct, but it is a shame that all the negative teachings were put in there also. Spirit has asked me to quote two passages out of the bible, which if all people who say they are religious lived by, then there would be no issues and the world would be a better place by far. If you live your life by these two quotes, then you are truly connected to the living God that surrounds you:

John 8:7   "He who is without sin among you, let him be the first to throw a stone at her."

Luke 6:31   "Do to others as you would have them do to you."

~Judge a man by his questions, rather than his answers~

WHO HAS THE ANSWERS?

More and more people are turning to Spiritualism to seek answers that no one else seems to be able to provide. Society is sick of the same hypocritical brain washing that they have been getting for generations from science, politics and religion. Individuals are now questioning the meaning of life more and more because of the state of the world and the position they find themselves in within it. People have been experiencing psychic phenomena since the beginning of time, having visions, knowing things, seeing angels, and communicating with those who have passed over. Yet again and again they have been told it is wrong if they experience these things or called liars by those who choose not to use their sixth sense. Just because someone you know can do these things and you cannot, does not make what they do wrong, or give you the right to judge them. Yes, there are people out there who are deliberate charlatans and are a disgrace, but then there are priests and so-called followers of God who are paedophiles and some of the cruellest people on the planet. I see many people trying to disprove the spiritual capability, however is a religious person who is really a child molester not a fake as well? I do not see a lynch mob trying to disprove their religion.

Politicians feed us just what they want us to know, and report stories in the news which they want us to believe but are not always necessarily the truth. They are all out for their own ends first and the country they are governing comes second. They are full of hype and propaganda which stirs people up and creates unrest and wars, all in the name of democracy. People are getting tired of this. They are getting tired of the rich getting richer and the poor suffering more and more. The money houses around the world are starting to collapse under the immense strain they have been under, and if one day money were to disappear that would be the best thing ever. All money does is create greed and without it there would be no criminal activity as such, because there would be no need. It would solve a lot of evils.

Science is a good thing in many ways, especially in medical research where the life-saving technology we have now is outstanding. Again though, scientific and pharmaceutical companies make a lot of money selling their products, which is not always the best cure for the individual concerned. Some scientists are starting to accept that there are certain phenomena that they cannot explain, such as Reiki and Spiritual Healing, and those who can communicate with the Spirit dimension. Then, there are those whose minds are still closed to all explanations that are not scientific. Well, they used to believe the world was flat, didn't they? The answers lie in all these forces working together in the future to combine their knowledge and expertise, in order to provide spiritual, scientific and medical help to those who need it.

Once people fully understand what causes the physical body and mind to become sick, then with the combined efforts of these great healing forces, the levels of disease and sickness we see in today's world would become a thing of the past. In the decades to come, a great understanding of spiritual and holistic approaches to curing illness will put the pharmaceutical companies out of business. They will no longer be needed to provide chemical medication which, in many cases, may help treat one symptom, but cause even worse problems with its side effects, which then develops into a vicious circle of combating the new symptoms with yet more drugs. The amount of money that these types of companies make from our ailments is astronomical, and therefore alternative healing and holistic methods are not being investigated or invested in as that would not be profitable for them. It is not about what is best for the sick individual, it is about generating profits for these companies, which in turn gives governments the most revenue. Again, it comes down to money, control and greed, all destroying Man and the planet.

However, there are growing numbers of people around the world who are becoming more and more disillusioned with the answers the medical professions currently provide. These people are aware of how damaging some medications are and the life limiting side effects that some drugs can give them. I know the medical and pharmaceutical professions are only providing what they have been taught, and that in the majority they are trying to help people with illnesses to either get better or to help control them. However, if they looked at an alternative approach, into what causes people to get sick in the first place, and then how to combat that, then our doctors and nurses, especially in the UK, would not be on the brink of collapse because of the immense pressure and strain they are under trying to treat sickness. If we learned to recognise what causes our mind and body to become sick, and acted to eliminate these factors, then the pressure on the NHS (National Health Service) and indeed on medical practices around the world would be greatly reduced.

There are also reasons to be optimistic about our future. Spiritual children who are being born now will take the world into the New Age and provide the answers of the future. Many such children have been born over the last hundred years or so. Some of you may recognize the terms of 'Crystal Children' or 'Indigo Children', you may even be one yourself. Over the next hundred years the birth of these types of children are set to explode! In the last twenty years there has been an increase, year on year, of these souls coming back, and right now there is a huge surge on the number of evolved souls that are incarnating into new born babies around the globe. Many of these children will grow into the next generation of 'Light Workers', prophets, healers, scientists, doctors, and mediums to guide our world in to a new era of understanding. Their existence is of utmost importance to the Earth, as their teachings and discoveries will be what saves Man and the world from self-destruction.

These children will be helped by beings from other dimensions which the human race will become aware of and interact with in the decades to come. They will only be successful if those who replace the current men of world power, are willing to listen, or if it is those people with evolved understanding who take the place of those in power now. If the crucial changes are not made within the next century then human existence as it stands now will cease to exist. It will depend on what those in power want more: the continual survival of the species or of money. Of course, they need to realise that if they choose commerce and money, greed and control, it will all be in vain, as what use is money when there will be no one left to spend it?

This is why we are entering a New Age, as people start to realise that they are spiritual beings on an incredible journey of discovery upon the Earth, and it is these individuals who will be responsible for saving the world.

~All that you are is around you~

THE NEW AGE

When was the last time you watched a sunrise or sunset and really appreciated its beauty and the miracle of what you were seeing? When was the last time you walked on a beach by the sea and took a moment to wonder what complex components of the Earth make it all possible? When was the last time you walked through the forest or through the mountains and appreciated the majesty of what surrounded you? When was the last time you looked up at the moon and stars and considered what importance they have upon planet Earth and in the universe? When was the last time you treated all living creatures on the Earth with equal love and respect, and with the realisation that all are as important as each other?

Or, like millions of others, do you just take it all for granted? Do you live each day in a blur of trying to squeeze in as much materialism as you can, not thinking beyond the next 'must-have' gadget, or fashion accessory? Do you walk down the high street with your head bowed deep in concentration and worry, or do you walk upright making eye contact with your fellow man, smiling at people and appreciating life?

This is the dawn of the New Age. The way humans have been living their life for a very long time now is wrong. So many of us take our planet, and all it provides, for granted without stopping for a moment to consider the greater meaning. Many of us have started to realise that unless we start working together and begin to understand that all living organisms on this planet are all interconnected by energies, we will cease to exist.

Have you noticed how many people have the 'Grow Your Own' bug now? Are you aware that people are looking at alternative medicines, spiritual healings, and holistic therapies as they try to find answers that the world is no longer providing? Time is running out for animal species that are close to extinction because they have been hunted to death, literally; for money, and groups of individuals are desperately working to try and stop this from happening.

All these things are happening for a reason. The people of today who are trying to make the world better by helping their fellow man or animal species in anyway are to be commended There is a greater force at work behind the scenes leading people on the Earth plane to do these things without the individuals really understanding why they feel compelled to do them. People from all walks of life are suddenly quitting their day job and way of life to throw themselves into helping others, even though the financial implication for them may be high, because they feel unfulfilled in their soul or they just cannot stand what is happening in the world any longer and want to try and 'do their bit' to help. If every single person did just one good deed, then in no time at all, the entire world would be on the road to recovery.

In the future, there are going to be many more who follow this path, there will be many more uprisings in oppressed countries to overturn dictatorships, there will be catastrophes with financial institutions around the world which will change the way we view money. There will be many more natural disasters that reshape countries and change the landscape of the Earth which will bring individuals closer together. Our planet is going through a major shift now which started with the Boxing Day tsunami in 2004. Many people believe 2012 was the year that all changes would have started, but this is not the case. Since 2004 there have been many severe natural disasters very close together; The earthquake in Haiti, the floods in Australia, where there have never been floods before, the earthquakes in New Zealand, the earthquake and tsunami in Japan to name but a few. These have not just been minor natural disasters, but major ones with many thousands of lives lost between them – it is like the Earth is rising up against all the abuse it has been getting and is trying to make its inhabitants realise that if we keep treating the Earth in the way we have been then this is how it is going to fight back!

Scientist talk about a new ice age that could affect our world, but the real issue everyone should be concerned with is that of global warming. The temperatures of the world are steadily rising because of the destruction of the ozone layer, through the gases that are released into our atmosphere by industry and transportation. The warming of the Earth is causing sea levels to rise as the ice caps melt at an alarming rate in our polar regions. If this continues at the rate that it has over the last ten years, then within our lifetime we will see islands disappearing under water all over the globe, especially low islands in the Pacific and Caribbean. Eventually, even here in England and the United Kingdom, places such as Cornwall, Devon, Plymouth and because of the flood plains, Somerset, would slowly be taken over by water. Many parts of England from Birmingham southwards would be affected in one way or another, and in the end, there would be no London anymore. This is a very real threat, but because it may not happen to this extent in our life time, many people of today shrug off the responsibility as being theirs and are happy to let the future generations worry about that, as long as they can continue enjoying the life and all the amenities they have right now. But it is our generation who can stop it. We need to put the reverse thrusters on now, or there may not be much land left for our great-grandchildren to live on.

Every gadget that has been invented to help make our life easier will be the cause of our destruction. Every microwave, fridge, television, mobile phone, car, or plane releases gases and radiation waves that are not good for us as human beings or for the Earth's atmosphere. These also cause human and animal sickness to those who are exposed to them. Have you noticed how many people are getting cancer now? Back in the 1940's & 1950's a small percentage of people contracted cancer, and that was mainly if they worked in mines or with substances that affected the lungs like asbestos. Those who came back from the wars, having been exposed to mustard gas and other chemicals, also developed cancers and lung diseases.

In the decades right through until the 1970's and early 80's there were not many obese people either, especially through the 40's, 50's and 60's, yet they ate all stodgy homemade cooking such as pies, pastry, cakes made with butter and lard, yet did not have weight problems, so how was this possible? There are those who will say there were not many cars back then, so people had to walk or cycle everywhere, which is part of it as nowadays people are a lot lazier and reliant on cars and public transport. Yet the exercise aspect of these decades is only a small fraction of it.

During this period there was not a fast food joint on every corner, there was no processed or fast microwave meals, there were less preservatives and additives being added to food in plastic packages in supermarkets, because all food was fresh. Animals were not fed steroids and hormone growth products to make them fatter quicker, chocolate was a rare treat not available to many, and the children drank milk or water, not the high sugar content fizzy drinks they do now. The reason inhabitants in the wealthier countries of the world are getting diseases and are becoming more and more obese, are because of a combination of all these factors. It stands to reason if you think about it carefully, that all the chemicals our animals are exposed to in our food chain will affect us, that all the preservatives and additives that are added in food to make them last will affect us, that all the chemicals in the plastic containers and wrappings our food comes in, will affect us.

The reasons people are getting more obese is not necessarily the amount that they are eating but *what* they are eating. If we all went back to a post-war lifestyle, obesity would become a thing of the past, and the incidence of these rampant cancers would be greatly reduced too. All the technological advancement, the fast food industries, the ability to get from one place to another quickly, and the chemicals we are exposed to are making us sick. If something drastic is not done about all these things over the coming years, then many people will die due to the cause and effect of 'Progress' and all that we have at our disposal, to make our life easier and more enjoyable, will in actual fact be the cause of our demise and the end of the Earth as we now know it. Inventors of ways that replace electricity, gas, fossil fuels, oil, and gadgets that are much greener, are being oppressed and in some cases, their reputation dishonoured, because these dominating industries would lose billions. There are many discoveries that are being made that would still enable us to enjoy most of the things we do today, but at a much less cost to the earth, and if these inventions are not allowed to be introduced, then all of humanity will continue to suffer for generations to come.

The New Age is going to be crucially important as we move into it, as the people who come to try and change things *must* succeed because if they do not, man will be signing his own death warrant. Spirit knows that there are many on the Earth plane who do not want to listen, because if they do and they change things, their profits will become less, and all those that rely on the gadgets and gizmos we have now would be in uproar. Yet if the world does not change then when everything comes to a cataclysmic end, they cannot say they did not have enough warning, or not enough messengers were sent trying to help.

~Do not feel lonely, the entire Universe is inside you~

OTHER DIMENSIONS

For decades there has been the question of other life forms existing apart from our own human one. Of course, other life forms exist and those who believe we are the only race alive in the universe are very naïve. Spirit knows that the prospect that other species exist apart from our own is a frightening one for many, however there will be interaction between us and other beings before the next century. These other races are far superior and more advanced than our own and they could be the difference between our planet surviving or not. There have been many conspiracy theories over the decades as well as the sightings of UFOs from around the globe, again as with the millions of children who have experienced past life memories, not all the people who have seen an UFO can be wrong can they? Yes, of course, some will have made it up to attract attention to themselves, but there are many which are genuine encounters and sightings. The reason it is covered up is because people panic. If an individual encountered something from another planet, they may be scared, but intrigued as well. If masses of people saw a being from another planet there would be pandemonium.

The Bermuda Triangle really does exist: there is a rip that opens under the right set of weather conditions. It is a magnetic force field that is created during intense electrical storms and exists for only a very short period of time, a bit like a black hole in space (although black holes are infinite). Many ships, and more recently planes, have been lost over the thousands of years due to this phenomenon. But the Bermuda Triangle is not the only place this phenomenon exists and there are a couple of points around the globe where these disturbances can take place under the correct extreme conditions. UFOs travel through light years, which is how they can transport themselves from one dimension to the next, and 'time' as we know it, in centuries and decades, does not exist in other dimensions in the universe. Their ability to travel depends on light energy and distance. I know many of you reading this will say this is utter nonsense and say that I am nutcase, however I can only write what is being dictated to me from a lot higher source. Over the next few decades the truth of what has been written here will start to become apparent and humans will communicate and interact with other beings from other planets.

There will be the discovery of a planet very similar to Earth, and two new moons within our solar system. People forget that we are only a small planet, in the grand scheme of things, and as well as trying to keep our species alive by changing our behaviours on Earth, we need to be aware of what is going on in space. Everyone is so busy with their own lives and scurrying around like ants that they do not give a second thought to what is floating around our solar system, and how important the other planets, the sun and moon are in relation to Earth's continued survival.

There are huge chunks of meteorites and space rock weighing many hundreds of thousands of tonnes. If one of them were to strike us in the wrong place, it would end the earth and all its inhabitants in an instant. The majority of people going about their everyday lives do not give any consideration to what is going on beyond their own existence, which is sad, as the wonders of the universe are a marvel to behold. Even how planets do not go floating off in to space, but stay where they are, rotating on their axis, is a miracle to behold really. The genius that is Professor Stephen Hawking has a great understanding of how all these things work, and we could learn a lot from physicists like him if we took the time to learn. But people do not seem to want to learn about things that do not affect them directly, like global warming, until some catastrophe were to happen, and they are forced to confront it. If we all took steps to acquire the knowledge and to take the action to nurture our Earth from within then we may still have a chance to save her.

Spirit will not give too much information in this book about the other dimensions, as this book is for people beginning their spiritual journey, and Spirit do not want to overload people with too much detail as it could be too much for many to process at this time. They have told me that they will give much more in-depth knowledge and teachings in the next book, and in the same way you would not give a new born baby a three-course meal to digest, Spirit will introduce this knowledge a little at a time, just like the weaning of a baby.

~It is health that is the real wealth, not pieces of silver or gold~

THE MIND, BODY AND HOLISTIC HEALING

In a previous chapter we talked about some of the reasons why people become sick, which is caused by external factors. We should now discuss other causes and what we can do to combat them. As we have said before, a person is a spiritual being in a physical body, and we are connected to the God Source by our ethereal cord. If you are not fully in tune with your higher self, and do not love and respect yourself and your body, it will become sick in some way. Those who truly value their life and totally love and respect themselves do not abuse their bodies or put substances in their bodies that should not be there. The human body is singularly one of the most magnificent and magical creations of all time. The punishment it can endure yet still function, is quite unbelievable, but so many of us still do not appreciate their living body or mind at all.

The largest human weight I know of was someone who weighed seventy-two stone. They were completely bed ridden and could not move, yet even under all that immense strain and pressure, their heart kept beating and everything kept working. How is that possible? On the other end of that spectrum the prisoners of war in the German concentration camps were so emaciated that their ribs were sticking out from their flesh, and yet again those that were rescued survived, even though *how* they could defy belief. It is logical that those who are obese, or who smoke, drink alcohol or take drugs will over time become sick, as the body can cope with this for a short period of time, but in the end you will suffer the effects of mistreating your body in these ways, yet because of the amazing ability of the human body, it can take many years for the body to become sick and for the effects to take hold.

There are many causes of diseases and sickness to the body, we discussed in an earlier chapter about the external forces, of the food we eat and the poisonous fumes we inhale every day, and the radiations we are exposed to. There are also hereditary and genetic factors that cause illnesses too, which are passed on through your genes and DNA. Those who smoke and put substances in to their bodies can really damage their health over time. The human body was not designed to cope with these man-made poisons and chemicals, as through evolution things like tobacco and alcohol, heroin and cocaine did not exist, so the body did not evolve and adapt to tolerate them, which is why they cause so much damage to those that use them.

The human body has an enough to contend with, just in its day to day survival without us adding to its burden by feeding it food it cannot break down and digest properly, or chemicals that it must work overtime to control to keep you alive. Human beings should eat food in little portions, as we have a small intestine which finds it very difficult to process animal fats, which is why it clogs up and can contribute to bowel and colon cancers, some bodies just cannot take it. There has been a nutrition revolution in the last decade or so, much more people are becoming vegetarian or vegan, some do it for the nutritional health it provides, others out of what they perceive to be spiritual growth. Spirit would like to clear a few things up about this, what a person eats is completely up to them, and no-one should be persecuted for this. They just want to state a few facts; humans are an animal species, the same as every other animal species, and they are not even top of the food chain, you only have to walk through a pride of lions unarmed to realise that fact pretty quickly. We have evolved as omnivores, and our teeth are designed for meat and plants. Becoming a vegan or vegetarian does not make you spiritually evolved, being spiritual has nothing to do with what you eat, it is purely a life choice.

When you become vegan, you must take a vitamin B12 supplement, which is a chemical, as vitamin B12 is not found in any fruit, nut, seed, vegetable or plant on the earth, it is only found in meat, fish, eggs and dairy products naturally. You do not have to consume animal flesh to receive the natural vitamin B12 that you need, but unless you want to take a chemical supplement, you do have to eat eggs or some form of diary. It is the way in which animals are treated for mass consumption that is the real issue, which has become barbaric in many cases, and this must change. As an example, if you lived in an Inuit society, in the artic conditions that they endure, you would have very limited choices for fruit and veg, as it cannot grow, and they have to eat produce from the sea in order to survive, it is only those of us that live in societies that have food at the touch of a button, that have the freedom of informed choices, but people forget this when they are judging others.

I used to eat a lot more meat than I do now, and now I find I do not want to eat it. I will still eat some white meat and fish, but when I eat red meat it makes me feel awful. I also have a difficult time now accepting the slaughtering of animals for our food, but I believe that is because I am now aware of our spiritual connection to all living creatures and that we are all connected by the same energy source. So, all these things can cause sickness in our body because of all the chemicals the animals are given, and all the chemicals plants are sprayed with, and all the chemicals used in processed food to make it last; yet there is one thing that can cause the most catastrophic of bodily ailments, pains and diseases; and that is the human mind...

The human mind is one of the most powerful and complex instruments of all time, not only in how it is physically constructed but also how it controls all your organs and intricate workings of your internal and external physical body. Most diseases and sickness start in the mind first, and then over time develop into physical symptoms, as this is the mind's way of telling you that you are out of tune with your higher self and that something is wrong which you need to pay attention to. Every single thought that you have every second of every day goes somewhere! It does not just fritter away into infinity.

Your conscious mind is the front runner, which is where thought is first created. When you are at work, typing away on your keyboard, it is your conscious mind that is being used on the job at hand. Your conscious mind is what you use when you are having a conversation with someone, doing your shopping, or thinking about what things you are going to tell your spouse off for. The conscious mind is in the 'here and now', it is in the present and it is one of the most essential components of your brain as it sends the signals to the appropriate parts of your brain that require immediate attention. Pain is felt in the conscious mind as it is in the here and now letting you know it is there. The subconscious, on the other hand, is also one of the most important parts of the brain as it is connected to your higher self-energy and where everything you have learnt and experienced over your lifetime is stored.

When you are at work typing on a keyboard, your conscious mind is concentrating on the words you are typing, yet your fingers are being controlled by your subconscious mind (if you can touch type), and you are not consciously looking at every key as you type, yet you can do it with ease. This is because the skill of touch typing that you learnt at school or college, is stored in your subconscious mind, and that is why you can use it without thinking about it when you need to. The subconscious mind never forgets anything, some things are buried very deep within it, for example those who have suffered abuse or traumatic events can sometimes not remember them freely because they have been buried that deep to protect the person, and only under therapy such as hypnosis can they be retrieved as hypnosis deals with the subconscious mind.

There are many people who dismiss hypnosis as nonsense without being aware that they are in a natural hypnotic state many times a day but do not recognise it as such. Let me explain what I mean. Have you ever travelled from one destination to another and wondered how you got there as quick as you did, as you do not consciously remember parts of the journey? This is a form of hypnosis as you drive without consciously thinking about the direction you are going in, especially if it is a route familiar to you. Another example is if you have ever sat down to watch something compelling on television, with a bowl of popcorn or a big bag of crisps then when you look down you discover the bowl is empty and you have eaten the lot without realising it? This is a form or hypnosis also, as you are transfixed on what you are watching you are not aware of what you are eating, and every single person alive has moments of hypnosis even though they are not consciously aware of what it is.

When driving and watching the cars in front and around you, checking your mirrors, or indicating to switch lanes, this is all done with your conscious mind, yet using your foot pedals, changing gear and steering is all done with your subconscious mind, and all the manoeuvres become as natural as breathing. When you learnt to drive all that knowledge was stored in your subconscious mind (your memory bank) and will never be forgotten. If you did not drive a car for five years, once you got back behind the wheel you would instinctively know what you needed to do, as you can never unlearn that which is stored in your subconscious. The only time this would change is with people who suffer severe head trauma and need to learn to walk or talk again, or those who get mind diseases such as Alzheimer's. Yet even those who have suffered severe head trauma and must learn to walk or write again, are able to re-learn these things because they have done it before. The ability and memory of the processes have been stored and are accessible again.

So, the first barrier is your conscious mind and then the place where all memories go is your subconscious, but it is not only your memories that are stored in your subconscious. All negative words, emotions, thought processes and traumas are stored there also. Every thought you have had, whether negative or positive, is first created in your conscious mind, if these thoughts are constantly repeated then the subconscious automatically stores them because it thinks that they are your beliefs and keeps them nice and safe for you, so you can recall them when you need them. The saying 'Be careful what you wish for' is very true, because if you keep having a negative thought or wishing for something to happen then your subconscious will work with your body and the universe to provide this. Even though your destiny cannot be changed, your life lessons can be determined by the choices and the mind-set that we have. Let me give you a recent example of this which happened to someone I have been close to for twenty-five years.

This person is a male in his early forties. It's fair to say that he is a bit of a tough guy and a 'man's man', as it were. He worked for a company for ten years, working his way up the ladder and had a few promotions along the way. Each promotion came with more responsibility, and by the end, his job totally and utterly controlled his life. His management position meant he was on constant call and would regularly do a hundred hours a week if you include all the time he spent on the phone having to sort out work issues. Even when he was at home the phone and responsibility never stopped, until he became completely stressed and burnt out.

He hardly saw his family and was completely unable to switch off and relax. The company he worked for could not see why this was an issue and had lost other employees because of it. In the last twelve months of his job, he started to get sick, had dizzy spells, pounding heart, panic attacks, life threatening high blood pressure and he started having time off work. When he went back to work the sickness would start again and over the months became so bad that he collapsed at work and had to be taken away in an ambulance.

I kept telling him that the symptoms were related to his stress and that if he kept ignoring it he would end up seriously ill or worse, but because he had a mortgage to pay and a family to support, he kept on. He used to say things like he wished he would have a heart attack, or a car accident which would then force the situation out of his control, so he could give up the job. What a horrible position to be in, and even worse, the way he was going, that was exactly what was going to happen to him. When he finally collapsed at work and took sick-leave, his company forced him to resign, which although a shock at the time, was the best thing that ever happened. Once he had left all his physical sickness disappeared completely. The continuous stress and unhappiness over the long period of time caused the symptoms to appear in his body, because the mind can only take so much, and when it has had enough it will give you the physical sickness as a way of making you aware that things need to change. Also, his negative thoughts and mind-set of him wanting the decision to be taken out of his hands happened, as in the end he had no control. I am just so pleased that it happened in a lot better way than him having a heart attack or a car accident.

What happened to my friend is a perfect illustration of the Mind-Body connection and Law of Attraction. When someone has suffered trauma or abuse for example, they can just try to carry on as normal and push it to the back of their mind (subconscious) and forget about it. However, traumatic experiences never just go away no matter how much we try to make them. When people refuse to confront or acknowledge negative emotions, or traumatic events, or when people stay in abusive relationships or situations that have a detrimental effect on them, over time all this unhappiness and negativity will try to escape from the mind through the body.

Depression is caused by continuous negative emotion and thought processes which, the mind eventually cannot cope with. One of the biggest causes of suicide is depression, because the mind is no longer operating rationally, and sufferers of depression find themselves in a seemingly inescapable prison of despair. Their depression is caused by years of negativity and the person refusing to acknowledge, or simply ignoring, the cause of their unhappiness, and not making the changes that will alter their state of mind for the better. In the cases of nervous breakdowns, the mind ceases to function logically, is unable to withstand any more, and has turned from depression to severe mental illness.

Some of the major physical symptoms of depression are panic attacks, shortness of breath, lethargy, continuous crying, paranoia, aches and pains especially in the stomach or back. Long term depression and stress can be physically debilitating and give rise to conditions like multiple sclerosis, fibromyalgia, stroke and heart attack. The symptoms may start quite mildly, as the mind tries to make you acknowledge the stress it is under, but will then manifest more serious symptoms, yet even if someone is suffering in this way, they will still refuse to see or change the root cause of their sickness. That is a person's choice, yet they could save themselves a lot of pain if they confronted the cause as soon as they start to feel it. If they cannot do it alone, then they should seek the help of a therapist who will help them, as I have done for many clients over the years.

Another consequence of blocking emotions and depression is self-medication. People will drink far too heavily or take drugs which they believe will make them feel better for a short while and make them forget their problems. Some people are not even aware they are doing this. When we talked earlier about obese people, even though some factors can be external, in many cases, such as in anorexia, the eating disorder is emotionally linked. I have treated many clients who use food as a substitute for something, or as a comfort to block a trauma out, in much the same way an alcoholic will reach for the booze.

It is so sad when people reach this point, yet if they were truly connected to their higher-selves or source, this would never happen. Society is very quick to judge the homeless, or alcoholics, yet we must never judge, as what you see in front of you are only the effects of a cause. You do not know what trauma has brought someone to their plight and we must try to help these people if they want it and bless them with love and move on if they do not. We could help someone if they would let us, yet until a person wants to change themselves, you cannot make them, and you can spend years of your own life trying to change and help somebody, inflicting great misery and unhappiness upon yourself.

As we move into this new age, even doctors and scientists are starting to acknowledge and investigate the mind-body connection, as they can see when the mind is not healthy and happy, the physical body is not either, yet when the mind is fixed the body will follow. This happens in many cases, yet for those who have let things go too far and had heart attacks or strokes, then some of the effects can be long term and irreversible. The connection between the two are very real and when more people start to accept this, the world will become a far healthier place. If changes are made to the external factors contributing to our bodies becoming sick, by the world becoming greener and stopping the pollution of our planet, then humans will start living for a lot longer. The original blueprint of the human body was designed to last for hundreds of years, not the fraction of this that it does now.

What many people fail to realise is that the natural approach to healing has been used for centuries and is not a 'namby-pamby' new age idea. Jesus Christ was one of the greatest spiritual healers this world has ever seen, because he was totally connected to his God source and higher self. Jesus knew that when those that came to him to be healed could be, as doubt about his abilities, or the source of his healing powers never entered his mind. So connected was he, that he could materialise food and wine from thin air because he simply accepted this ability.

There was also a man called Sai Baba who died in 1918, who is regarded as a type of saint because he performed some of the 'Miracles' that Jesus could too, again because he was in complete unison with his higher self and connection to the Creator energy source. Witches used to be burnt at the stake and drowned in rivers because of their ability to use natural plants and herbs that grow in all countries to treat the sick. Many so-called witches could make natural poultices that were effective in the treatment of tuberculosis, which was rife in those times, as well as making infusions and remedies for many ailments. It is the same today as it was then, but just more civilised depending on which country you live in.

Some countries still kill mediums and healers because they believe they are working with the 'Devil', which of course is absolute nonsense as they are just using a natural born ability that is available to everyone should they take the time to investigate it. All-natural herbs, plants and flowers that grow on the Earth are here to provide remedies for sickness, which is why they were created and put here in the first place. The reason Jesus, and other great messengers and healers have been persecuted for their beliefs and abilities, is because of one simple factor. Fear.

Fear is the key factor that holds human and spiritual evolution back, for those who do not understand something new or unfamiliar tend to fear it instead. Witches and other healers down the centuries who have worked 'miracles' were persecuted instead of being appreciated for the gifts they gave to others. With the men of power, if someone comes along who can offer another solution to the one that currently makes them a lot of money and gives them control over millions of people, then they will reject it completely and if they then fear that person is being listened to and believed, they will make sure that their ways are adhered to by whatever means necessary.

Unfortunately, in our modern age, most of us are brought up to believe that only chemical or man-made medicines can help us, as many companies make astronomical amounts of money making us believe that. Because of their worldwide monopoly in pharmaceuticals and medical research, these companies will usually dismiss or ridicule anything that might be labelled 'Alternative Medicine'. However, if millions of people investigated holistic medicines and treatments seriously, then these companies would lose billions in revenue. This fear stops them from even looking into alternative homeopathic solutions.

Spirit also understands and appreciates that some man-made medicines such as penicillin and vaccines for childhood diseases have saved countless lives by their invention, yet if they explored natural medicines too, then a lot of unnecessary side effects and complications caused by synthetic medication would be stopped, which would benefit everyone concerned.

There are many alternative and holistic treatments which you can use to help keep your body and mind healthy and happy. Healing such as Reiki and reflexology helps to align your energies, clear blockages in your energy centres (Chakras) and keeps your external energy force field (Aura) vibrating correctly which will protect you from sickness. Practices such as reflexology and acupuncture have been around for centuries and in countries like Japan and China they are widely used and highly regarded. The Japanese and Chinese particularly understand the mind-body connection like no other, and if you have ever been to see a Chinese practitioner, you may have been as amazed as I was when she told me what symptoms I had been getting at the time, and what had caused them, just by looking at my tongue!

This happened years ago as I was starting on my journey of self-discovery and made me look more closely at these alternatives to orthodox Western medicine, because I could not believe that someone could tell what was wrong with you by looking at your tongue. A GP later confirmed by conventional blood tests exactly what the Chinese practitioner had told me. With Reiki you can feel the energy shifts inside your body whilst you are on the table. You can feel things 'moving' inside of you, which is a very strange sensation when you first have it done, and some people feel heat or cold or pressure of some sort. The amazing thing is that when you have had a session such as Reiki, you have an overwhelming sense of calm and wellbeing. Some doctors say that it is merely the 'placebo effect', and that it is mind over matter, which to some degree could be true, however you actually *feel* the sensations in your body at the time. Even sceptics who have undergone a session have said they felt the benefits of such treatment too, so it cannot be dismissed as just mind over matter.

Crystals, whose tremendous healing powers have been used for thousands of years, are also helpful in curing human ailments. There are even certain crystals that if you place around your home and work place will absorb the electrical magnetic impulses and radiation from your electrical devices, so they do not affect you. The best crystal for absorbing this type of negative radiation is black hematite; Obsidian will also absorb some of this but can also absorb negative emotions extremely well. A few years ago, I suffered from recurring infections and abscesses in my teeth and gums. One night, the pain was so intense that I wanted to remove my head so it would stop, anyone who has ever had bad dental pain will know what I mean! I had a piece of a crystal called fluorite, and I placed it on my jaw line while I tried to sleep. Now, this crystal is typically the colour of brown sugar, yet in the morning when I woke, the crystal was mainly white and the pain had gone. The crystal had absorbed the infection.

Some people reading this will think I am making this up or off my rocker, but it is the absolute truth, and from this point onward I started researching the healing power of crystals. They are amazing, and I would ask everyone reading this to learn more about the different types of crystal and their ability to help you. This is why Spirit World is so passionate about bringing the two worlds of medicine and healing together, because if you combined scientific medicine with the holistic therapies the healing that would take place would change the world.

I am sure you have all heard of the 'placebo effect' where scientists have tried to prove that 'mind over matter' can be a powerful healing tool. In various studies and experiments patients are told that they have been injected with a powerful drug, whereupon they have recovered and felt better, even though what they were injected with was clear saline solution. As stated in the previous chapter, the mind is the most amazing healer on the planet, and this proves that when you truly believe something positive, or that something has healed you, then your body will respond to it. The scientific community is investigating this phenomenon as they search for answers to help them understand just what the human mind is capable of.

There are many cases involving people who have been in horrific accidents and have severed their spinal cord, the damage being clearly visible in X-rays, and have been told that they would be paralysed for life. Yet those same people have walked out of the hospital months later, astonishing all medical professionals who declare it a 'miracle'. It is a miracle of sorts, it is the miracle of the human mind, because what the mind will believe, the body can achieve. As we move forward in the next hundred years, more and more people will start to realise and use the power that is stored within to heal themselves from the inside. This, coupled with holistic healing and other alternative treatments, will totally change Mankind's view on sickness and disease, and that would be a wonderful achievement.

~When all else is lost, only the future remains~

HOW CAN WE HELP OURSELVES?

The best way to help ourselves is to remain focused firmly on the present. When you live in the past, especially if you are bitter or angry about experiences you have had, then this is extremely detrimental to your wellbeing. When you fret and worry about what is coming in the future and become stressed about what has not even happened yet, this is very bad for you too. The way to connect to your higher self, becoming totally at one with your mind and body, is to be fully living in the present moment. Once you are on the path to self-discovery you will understand that the answers to all your questions are accessible from within yourself and that by living day by day in the moment, you will live and experience your life and not merely exist within it.

You must become the driver in your life, instead of the passenger, and therefore gain total control. So many people waste their lives by living in the past or worrying about the future, forgetting to live in the present and enjoy what is in their lives right now. We need to understand that we are where we are in our lives right now for a reason, and that we need to appreciate what we have got right now, not what we think we should have, or how we think our lives should be at this point. It is what it is, and if you are not happy in your life in some way, then being fully present in the moment will allow you to examine what has brought you to where you are now, and that may reveal some uncomfortable truths for you.

However, as painful as it may be, we can only ever progress in life when we have held the mirror up to ourselves, been completely true to ourselves and accepted full responsibility for our own actions. I see so many people during the course of my work who Spirit will try to guide through me, yet because they will not be true themselves, or refuse to accept that they or their situation needs to change, they remain trapped in a negative cycle. Sometimes Spirit becomes as frustrated as I am, when certain people have come back to me once a year for several years, and they are still in the same negative position they were in when they first came to see me. They fear change or will not accept what they need to do to make their lives better.

Sometimes I become upset because I know, with each passing year, that their state of mind becomes worse, and each year there is an added physical ailment that has presented itself and I know that they are doing a lot of damage to their physical and emotional health. Yet Spirit says to me when I become frustrated, that I cannot make anyone face the truth and to make changes, and I should only hope that eventually they see the light before it is too late for them. But in the meantime, I just have to continue trying to guide them in the right direction.

You cannot change the past and reliving it constantly, or picking over the bones of negativity within it, will do you great harm. When you fully understand the meaning of life and accept it, you will understand that certain past experiences are what have brought you to your present. If your past has been full of what you perceive as mistakes, then learn from them and let them go. You have not really made any mistakes, you made decisions based on what you thought was correct for you at that time in your life. If those decisions had a detrimental effect on you, then you know not to repeat them in your present or in your future. Mistakes are experiences, and the lessons you have learned from them, are what you asked for before you returned to the earth plane in the body you occupy right now.

Some of your experiences will have occurred from your life choices as well as what lessons you are destined to learn here. Spirit World cannot make this next message any clearer: If you hold onto negative experiences from your past, experiences that make you angry or fill you with hate towards another, you will, in time, become very ill. Hatred and anger are the biggest causes of psychological sickness, which in turn can become major physical illnesses that will kill you. If you find this hard to believe, then think about yourself or someone you may know who has suffered hurt and trauma in their lives and are filled with bitterness and vengefulness. Is that person fit and well, with a healthy body and mind?

If you are being completely honest, the answer to this question is bound to be: No. Those of us who have had trauma in our lives, and are filled with sadness as a result, will experience periods of depression that result in physical illness. So many of us, though, do not make this connection, so millions of human beings are unaware that the negative thoughts and emotions they have been carrying round with them for years are *actually* the cause of their physical illnesses. Once the physical sickness symptoms are exhibited in the body, our current approach is to cure the symptoms, not the cause, but until we uncover the root cause of our illness, a cure will be impossible. You may be able to control the symptoms for a while, but in the end, they will get worse or another sickness will emerge elsewhere in the body. The other sad fact is that once the physical illness has progressed too far, then even if you have therapy to eliminate the negative root causes, you can be left with the effects forever. The way to overcome and release hatred and anger is to forgive. I know that we feel some crimes are unforgivable, especially those against our children, and if we have been severely hurt by someone the thought of forgiving them seems out of the question.

What you *must* realise is that when you forgive someone for the way in which they have hurt you, you are not condoning their actions, and neither should you remain in a relationship or situation where someone is hurting you. When you forgive, you are releasing that part that is causing you hatred, anger, sadness, fear or guilt, and by releasing what is causing you these negative emotions, you are taking back the control of your own life. As long as you hold onto hate, or keep experiencing negative emotions, the person that caused you to feel this way still has a hold over you. Even if you have not seen them for twenty years, you are still allowing them to control your life, because you continue to live with the negative influence that they caused you. By truly forgiving someone who has hurt you, you are starting the healing process within yourself and when you let all that pent up anger and hurt go, you will start to see a big difference in the way you think and feel about things, only by attaining this can you be at peace and happy from deep in your soul. Forgiveness does not happen overnight, and it can take a long time of self-work in order to achieve it. I speak from personal experience of this, so I know how very difficult it can be. However, if you can master it, you will be free.

To help ourselves in our life's journey we need to face up to reality, we need to confront problems or the causes of our unhappiness head on. We need to be true to ourselves first and foremost, we need to hold up the mirror and admit whether the negative situation we find ourselves in is of our own making, or indeed that we have contributed to it by our thoughts, deeds, actions or behaviours. If we are abusing our body in some way by the substances we are putting in to it then we need to stop, and if we know our body is trying to tell us something because it is sick in some way, then we need to face up to the actual causes and tackle them because they will not go away, they will only intensify over time. If you are unhappy or sick because of another person who makes you feel this way, then leave that relationship now.

You can make all the excuses you want for not leaving a situation that is causing you continuous distress or unhappiness, however the only person who will continue to suffer is you. If you are willing to put up with that and accept the consequences of your actions, then that is your choice and your free will which you were born with. But if you are reading this now and are in a negative situation, please know that life is much too short to live unhappily, and that as soon as you start to make the changes to your life, the universe will respond and open up to you, but you must take the first step or the universe thinks you just want to continue receiving more of the same, because you do not take any action to change it.

~Be careful what you wish for~

THE LAW OF ATTRACTION

Many of you will have heard of the 'Law of Attraction' as there are many self-help books and videos out there about it, yet unfortunately a lot of these can be misleading as they talk about a world of abundance, yet they concentrate mainly on the manifestation of money. They also lead you to believe that whatever you want to achieve is possible, and that you can be whoever and whatever you want to be as long as you make dream boards and change your mind to a positive way of thinking, living your life continually repeating positive mantras that in the end will be absorbed in to your subconscious and then made a reality.

Today's younger generation has been raised to believe that they can achieve great riches, be successful and that it is their natural right to be able to gain this easily. Many young people see celebrities on the television and want to copy them, envying what they have and believing that this will bring them happiness. They wish to live a life of fantasy, yet they are setting themselves up for great failure and disappointment 90% of the time. They waste their life striving for fame and fortune when many do not have the talent, and those who do have genuine abilities struggle for many years while trying to become successful and, even then, raw talent does not guarantee you success.

The huge technological achievements of the last few decades have meant that millions of people's jobs and careers have been lost as human beings have been replaced by machines and robots. These machines can do the work of a thousand men in a fraction of the time, which is great for productivity but not so good for struggling families with many mouths to feed. Manual labour has been steadily dying out in many industries such as mining, steel and shipping, the young people of today seem to place little value or have no understanding of what 'real' work is. They feel that being on the television or becoming famous is the way to achieving all they desire.

What is also of a great concern is that while machines and robots come to replace human beings in the work place, if this continues at the rate it is, in the next hundred years there will hardly be any professions left that a machine cannot perform, yet the world's population is continuing to increase. If things continue in the way that they are, we will have a situation where we have billions of people on the planet but not enough employment vacancies for them, so how will the population feed themselves, and where will they live? How will they afford to survive on a planet that increasingly focuses on money, power, fame and materialism? How will your grandchildren manage under these kinds of living conditions? Have you even stopped to think where all this is heading?

Right now scientists and the human race marvel at the scientific advancement and how robots and machines can do these wonderful things that make our life so much easier so we have more free time to pursue whatever we want, but how will our great-grandchildren feel if they are born into a world of struggle because robots and machines have taken over the job opportunities that they need to provide for their own families? There needs to be measures put in to place now to stop this happening in the future or the world will be in very big trouble indeed.

So, the Law of Attraction is supposed to bring you whatever you want so long as you have a positive attitude and keep believing you are going to be successful and focusing upon whatever your hopes and dreams are. It is said that by following these guidelines everything will come to you. I don't like to be the bearer of bad news, but this is not how the Law of Attraction works. Spirit has become increasingly frustrated by the misrepresentation of something that is potentially accessible to everybody, and by how the self-styled, self-help gurus are themselves cashing in and making lots of money by targeting what they know most people want to achieve, namely money and power, and claiming that by following certain steps people can have all this and more. Not true.

Nor will you gain immense wealth, power and success through the Law of Attraction if it not your destiny to do so. Those who ultimately become successful or famous do so because it is their destiny, combined with all the hard work they have put in. You are more likely to succeed in life when what you are pursuing is out of passion and love, not for the sole purpose of making as much money as you can. If you are here to develop spiritually through lessons of hardship, strife, or are perhaps repaying a Karmic debt which is money related, then no matter what you do, you will not attain it in this lifetime unless you have truly learnt that lesson and become more financially secure later in your lifetime. One of my lessons on the Earth plane has revolved around money because in one of my previous incarnation as a man, I gambled my whole life away and lost everything. Yet even up to the point of my death in that previous lifetime I was still trying to win, and recoup some of what I had lost, which was impossible of course.

Every business venture I have tried during my life up to now has failed and cost me a lot in the process. It is only now as I am truly starting to wake up and understand the true meaning and lessons of life that I am realising where I have been going wrong. How many of you reading this have tried and failed repeatedly to make money in your life, either through employment or your own business ventures? Tried get rich quick schemes? Gone from one money making project to the other, just trying to have a breakthrough with something that would bring you the financial success you so desperately desire?

That is precisely where we have been going wrong: the more you need and focus on money, the more you will push it away. Yet the more you struggle financially here on the Earth, the more desperate you become, the more you will try to embark on schemes to bring you money, and invariably each and every one will fail which will leave you feeling more miserable and dejected each time until in the end you give up. The only way to change this is by following the true path of the Law of Attraction, and the real force behind the Law of Attraction is Love, not money or materialism.

For the Law of Attraction to truly work for you, the decisions and choices that you make in your everyday life must be driven by love. Love is the highest emotion and therefore it vibrates at the highest energy level possible. When you vibrate and project love, a positive mental attitude will follow automatically, as it is not something you will have to keep convincing yourself of until it sinks into your subconscious mind. When you are doing something you love, it makes you happy from within which releases endorphins in your brain that flood your body with the 'Feel Good Factor'. These make you feel exhilarated, a bit like jumping out of a plane and the adrenaline rush you get as you take that leap of faith, for that is what believing in the Law of Attraction is: it is a leap of faith.

Another factor in the Law of Attraction is your attitude towards life, and how positive or negative you allow yourself to be. We have all had to do jobs that we do not particularly like, so we can provide for our families, however it is how we allow that to affect us that determines whether we attract something better or stay stuck in the same routine and just complain about how awful it is. Accepting your situation and being at peace with it will open the door to better things, so if you are doing something currently that you really do not want to be doing but feel right now that you have no other choice because you have responsibilities, then accept that and make peace with it. Accept it and know in your heart and soul that this is just a temporary solution and that you will start moving towards a job or in a different direction as soon as the time is right.

When you make this pact with yourself all the negativity you have been holding onto will disappear and your state of mind will become clearer. Then set yourself realistic goals to start moving towards what you want, not out of a desire for money, but out of the love and passion for whatever it is you want to do. As you do this the Law of Attraction will come into play and start to work with you and guide you along the way. Only by having a true love and passion for something will you be able to work with the Law of Attraction to help it manifest itself in your life. At the same time, do not forget that if something is not your destiny then the true deep love and passion for it will not actually be there in the first place. There may be a desire and strong leaning toward that area, and you may even want something so much and with such power that you attain it, but once you have it, you are still not happy.
The reason for this is because you have achieved it for the wrong reasons, and the one person whom you cannot fool in the end is yourself.

When you have a positive mental attitude to life, there will still be challenges in your life that you must face because they may be part of your blueprint, however a person who is vibrating love and always takes the 'glass is always half full' attitude toward life, will always come out the other side of a crisis with a greater understanding of themselves and the situation. They do not become lost in the negative emotions, therefore even though they may have had to overcome a crisis they do not continually attract negative happenings because of their mind-set. Yes, the Law of Attraction works negatively as well as positively. Let me give you an example.

Have you ever got up in the morning and stubbed your toe as you are getting out of bed? How many of you have noticed that when you do this that annoying first incident sets a precedent for the rest of the day? So, you stubbed your toe getting out of bed and you omit a few swear words and it makes you a little grumpy! Then you drop your toast on the floor, butter side down of course! Then the traffic is a nightmare when you are trying to get to work, or you miss your bus or train by a minute? When you get to work you have to deal with an irritable boss or irrational customers? Then by mid-afternoon you have got a thumping headache and are feeling hard done to and completely out of sorts with yourself? Sound familiar?

This is because when that initial negative event occurs we become annoyed and irritable, but unfortunately because we are concentrating on the negative thing that happened we then attract more of the same as we are vibrating on a low negative level. We can attract negative stuff for days just because we stubbed our toe getting out of bed one morning, and before you know it, the washing machine has packed up, the car's got a flat tyre, and the dog has swallowed your keys! You get my drift.

By focusing only on what is negative and perpetuating it by telling everyone all the bad things that have happened your audience then start to sympathise with you. By this time, you really are on your soap box, and all that negativity is churning up and coming off you in waves, so the universe sends you more because you must want it as you are concentrating on it so much. When these things happen to you, you need to realise what is happening and stop it straight away. When you stub your toe acknowledge that it hurt, call yourself silly, and then think of something that is happy or pleasant to take your mind off it. Start whistling or singing to raise your vibration, or think of something good, or a fun event that you plan to attend and concentrate on that instead.

I know this may sound ridiculous, but if you adopt these methods of moving your focus from the negative to the positive, you will see a difference in what happens to you very quickly. It is not what happens to us, but the way in which we deal with it that determines our mind-set and our life. I know I have used a fairly light and basic example to prove my point, but by focusing on negative events and experiences in your life, and by having a constant negative belief and mind-set, the only things you will draw to yourself is unhappiness and in many cases sickness too. This is the Law of Attraction when it is working against you, but it can only send you the energy you are vibrating on. Where we start off in life, or where we are right now is not the place we will end up. Life is ever changing, and your life can change for the better within sixty seconds. Just hold on to that thought if where you are right now in life is a struggle and you cannot see a light at the end of the tunnel. Start helping yourself, baby steps, one day at a time and you will reach your destiny in the end, we all do.

Remember the true Law of Attraction is Love, which is quite significant really, as the True Meaning of Life is Love also. To be in total balance with yourself and the world, all that you do in life has to have love as its origin and if this is the case then you will be vibrating at such a high level that all you will attract is more of the same. So-called good luck is manifested because you are vibrating with a love and a passion for something, and when someone receives a lucky break it is because this is their destiny and the Law of Attraction is working with them to achieve it. Over the years there have been many people that we have admired or looked up to because of their success, which is sometimes only achieved after a great struggle for them. A few people that Spirit wishes me to mention who were driven by love and a passionate belief in something were, Nelson Mandela, Ghandi, Martin Luther King Jnr, Emmeline and Christabel Pankhurst, Henry Ford, Albert Einstein and Alexander Fleming.

Now, apart from Henry Ford, none of these pioneers achieved great riches in monetary terms, yet through their love, belief and dedication they changed the lives of millions in their own ways and every single person alive today still uses or benefits from what they invented or believed in. Great success and achievement is rarely measured by money, as you cannot take it with you when you die, however in today's world it seems that so many truly believe that success can only be measured by how much you have in the bank, or how famous you are which actually are the least important things in a person's life.

There are those alive today who have achieved great wealth through what they love, and the one-person Spirit wants me to mention here is Sir Richard Branson. What sets Richard Branson apart was not an overwhelming desire to become a billionaire with a hugely successful global business empire, but his love and passion for music that saw his first success. Richard loved and still loves music, starting off with a small shop selling records which was then built it up to the mighty and highly influential Virgin Records. With his natural aptitude for business and entrepreneurial flair he then diversified into many other industries, but his original success in the music industry was his destiny and was born not out of how many millions he could make, but out of his love for music. That is why Richard Branson has been so successful, working tirelessly to nurture and grow what he really loved. He learnt from his mistakes, he was true to himself always and he used his brilliance in business to his advantage, so because of this the Law of Attraction worked with him and brought him more of the same.

To be truly successful in this life, you must be driven by love and the passion for something and then you must work hard to achieve it, and only then will the Law of Attraction open up its magnificent abundance to you. In most cases when you are doing what you really love, financial security will follow, even if it takes some time. A couple of examples right now are the two very talented British musicians Ed Sheeran and Sam Smith.

Both Ed and Sam tried for years to get noticed and both worked extremely hard to get a break. They both are driven by their true love and passion for music and because it is their time everything is starting to fall in to place. Sam Smith perhaps unknowingly has put it out to the universe with the lyrics of his song, "Money on my Mind" that has got him noticed, which is not a coincidence by the way and Spirit wants me to quote him, as it reiterates everything they are trying to teach us all in this chapter. "I don't have money on my mind, money on my mind, I do it for, I do it for the love".

~The Past can't see you, but the Future is listening~

YOUR FUTURE IS UP TO YOU

Where you go from this point in your life is entirely your choice. Will you live the life you have been living even though it may be making you unhappy or even ill? Or will you listen to the teachings that Spirit has shared in this book, and start taking the small steps towards making changes which will benefit your state of mind and body? As Spirit has continually stated throughout this journey we have embarked on together, your destiny is already written, but how you get there is through your own choices and decisions you make along the way, and through the challenges and experiences you have encountered and, in some cases, endured.

It matters not how bleak or hopeless your life may seem to you right now, because if you have learnt anything from this book you will now be starting to change the way you view your situation and the world, and you will have a seed of hope that has been planted in your soul that will germinate and grow until it blooms brilliantly and beautifully, nurtured by love, passion and faith. There may be things I've written that you cannot accept or agree with yet, which is perfectly fine, as you will absorb and act on this information when you are ready. As your understanding develops through the rest of your life and as your soul evolves, then other teachings will reach inside of you and make their presence felt.

The evolution of the soul takes many lifetimes to complete and you must not put yourself under any pressure to make radical changes in your life that you are not ready for yet, just the act of knowing what they are and being true to yourself will start the process for you. Everything in life happens at the correct time it is meant to, not a second before and not a minute after, and if you try to force things before they are ready you will be met with resistance and obstacles. Be aware that is what they are and bide your time, as when it is the right time for changes, all falls in to place as if by magic. If you are dissatisfied with your life as it stands, accept it is what it is for now and make your peace with that, then by being totally truthful to yourself decide what it is that you want from life and where your love and passions lie, and then start making the changes to achieve them. Only by aiming for something out of love can you achieve that higher vibration and positive mind-set that will allow the Law of Attraction to open to you and to work with you while you move forward in your life.

If you are holding on to trauma or negative experiences from your past that are interfering with you living your life in a happy and fulfilled way, you must not continue to ignore it, if you cannot do it alone you must seek the correct help to eradicate the negativity. I cannot stress how important and potentially life-saving doing this can be for you, for if you continue to live your life as a victim, repeating and amplifying the negative patterns that this creates, you will cause your mind and body great and sometimes irreversible damage. My advice is to find a therapist who is NLP (Neuro Linguistic Programming) trained, as well as hypnotherapy and if possible, regression-trained also. Not all root causes of negativity were created in this lifetime, so you need a practitioner who can cover it all in the same way I do with my clients. Once you have eliminated your negative thoughts, deeds, actions or behaviours from the root, they will not return, and you will start off with a clean slate from here.

You must also live your life completely in the present, do not worry about the future, as it will happen regardless of how much you concern yourself with it. Do not remain in the past and if you are, eliminate the cause of that so you are free to live in the here and now as life was intended to be lived. Enjoy and savour each moment of the present: when your child draws you a picture at nursery, or you have a day out to remember, remain ever present and fully here. Life passes by so quickly and the days roll into weeks, months and years in the blink of an eye, and it is totally up to you if you make the most of every day or whether you get through each day miserable and unhappy with your lot. The saying 'Live every day like it's your last' is completely correct, as we don't know when it will be, so it is up to us to make the most of every day and to view life as a gift we have been given not as a burden we have to bear.

Do not be bitter or resentful of experiences or events that have brought you to where you are in your life right now, as without them you would not have learned some of the great lessons you have even if you find that difficult to accept. You are where you are right now as that is where your choices have led you, and where some of the experiences that were pre-destined have led you, however where you go from here is entirely up to you, and when you acknowledge that truth, your life will truly be what you make it.

As Professor Dumbledore says to Harry in Deathly Hallows part 2, "Do not pity the dead, only pity the living, especially those that live without love". I use this quote because I believe the author of these amazing books is a prime example of a life of struggle that turned around through her love and positivity. JK Rowling was living a life of poverty and hardship when she was writing Harry Potter as a single mum in a cramped flat. When she created Harry, it was her love and passion for what she was doing that spurred her on, she sent the manuscript to many publishers who did not think it was worthy of notice, JK was not thinking about how many millions she could make if someone published it, just how many children she could reach, who would be as enthralled and excited by Harry's adventures as she herself was, and I can only imagine the hurt and dejection she must have felt as again and again it was rejected, yet all of us who has read these books can see JK Rowling's genius and brilliance in what she created.

Look at where she is now, she has abundance beyond her wildest dreams and I don't just mean in monetary terms, this is where love, faith, passion, hard work and endurance have brought her, this is the Law of Attraction in full use, and for me in my physical life JK Rowling greatly inspires me. As I am drawing to a close on the book, once Spirit has left and I read what has been written I wonder if I will ever have this book published, the niggling doubts try to surface in my mind, and I have to push them away, and have utter faith that this book will reach everyone it is meant to by whatever means that takes, because I have written this book out of my love, passion, belief and faith in Spirit World, which when I listen and follow their infinite guidance, always lead me to the correct path. They will lead you too if you open your heart and mind to them and connect to them and to your higher self, they will never steer you wrong I can promise you that. There are a couple of guidance meditations at the end of the book to help you connect. Go out there and make a life for yourself that you can be proud of, and live each day true to you always, the true meaning of life is love. Love of others but most importantly love of self. If you can live your life secure in this knowledge and connected to that vibration you will have abundance in all areas of your life that are important to you.

Love & Blessings to you all.

Judith x

A LAST MESSAGE FROM SPIRIT

My name is Lazarus and I am currently the main guide of the Spiritual Teacher known as Judith Hindle. I started working with Judith in 2012 and her development has been very rapid from now to then. Judith's progression had been very hampered in the past by her continuous need to question everything, in some ways this is good as she challenges every decision and suggestions so she does not become a sheep, yet even though she knows what we say to be the truth within her heart, she has continually fought against it which has made her own path very difficult and troubled. Judith went to see a Spirit Artist in 2011 and the artist drew me, and Judith thought she had made a mistake because she had not met me herself yet then, when I stepped forward in 2012, Judith then realised her drawing had indeed been correct.

I come from the time and place you know as Atlantis in your world, and I was an Elder at a time when all communication was telepathic, deed was thought, and words were not needed. Manifestation of objects through thought were commonplace and there was no sickness of mind or body as these things did not exist because everyone was connected to their Higher Self and therefore to their God Force Living Spirit Energy always.

People lived for hundreds of years then, as there were no toxins in the body or in the atmosphere, because crystals provided all healing energies and light vibrations. As with all cycles of time on the Earth plane, Atlantis came to an end as the younger generation that was born wanted to venture out and discover the world and beyond, and inevitably with that came the need for domination and rule, for power and for greed, and again this was the downfall of that time, the same as it has been the destructive force many life cycles over, and it is here again now in your world. In Spirit World I am a member of the wise counsel and I sit amongst many beings who have evolved much higher than I and divulge their infinite wisdom and knowledge to those of us who have dedicated our existence to the guidance of those upon the Earth plane who can communicate with us. There is much concern in the Spirit World regarding the state of your Earth, as for many years we have sent messengers to warn you about the destruction of your planet from your industrial inventions, yet only a few are willing to listen and even fewer to try and stop the damage. Through the Spirit Channel known as Judith Hindle and through many more messengers like her, we in Spirit are sending as much information and warnings as we can to try to get those in power that will listen, to change their behaviours now before it is too late. The Earth is heading for another Polar Shift, which means the North Pole and the South Pole will switch positions again, and when this happens it causes catastrophic loss of life both in the human kingdom and in the animal and plant kingdom also. These shifts have happened many times over the billions of years the Earth has been alive, however because of the population of the world now and because of the industrial progress of the earth, the next shift really will be what you perceive as Armageddon. There will be very few that survive it, and only those that are spiritually attuned, or have a connection to their Higher Self will come through the other side, however the Earth will be a very dark place for many hundreds of years in the aftermath of such an event. There is still time to stop this from happening, but only if those who control the world come together and put their need for money, greed and power to one side and focus instead of the survival of the human race and all other species on the planet Earth.

There will be beings from other dimensions sent to help you, but as things stand now you will probably try to eliminate them or see them as a threat, they are not. They are much more evolved than humans and therefore can assist as they are more advanced than you can possibly imagine in all ways. As things are right now, and if you reject all help and continue to pollute the planet at the rate you are now, the next Polar Shift will take place within the next two hundred earth years. This will sound like a long time to many of you reading this, and you will say that you will be long gone by then, so it is of no concern to you; yes, it is. As future generations live on, those who helped create this Armageddon will be reincarnated to experience it once it happens, as that is the Karma that will be created. Do not think that you can behave as you want to now in this lifetime and that there will be no consequence. Do not think that once you die, what you have done here no longer matters, because it does, and every single living being leaves a soul footprint on the Earth plane. If you are one of the powerful men of the world who are contributing to the destruction of this planet from your power and greed, then do not be under the misconception that you will escape the consequences of those actions in your next incarnations, as that is not how the universal laws operate.

It is not yet too late to change the course of destruction that the Earth is heading towards, but the difference now is that it is the Governments, Royalty, Leaders, Heads of State and men of power that need to make the decisions and act to stop this. There are many individual people on Earth who are in touch with their Higher Self, who know what needs to be done to halt this devastation, but they are lone voices or without the power to put the changes in to action. It is only those that are in these positions who can now make the decisions that will bring these changes in to being, as a collective force. When governments and leaders make the laws that govern a country then people will follow, yet when people want change and the Governments do not then this causes anarchy. The changes need to come from the top and then flow down to the masses, as this is the only way to change mind-sets that exist right now. In days that have passed, a king used to ride out to battle and lead from the front; when he did this his people listened to him and respected him as he was prepared to put his life on the line to defend what he believed in, and was prepared to die to protect his people from those that would seek to rule them, or to destroy them. It is time for the kings, queens and rulers to lead those they rule once more, to unite with the people, to listen to the people and to stand up for what is right for those that depend on them. It is time for these leaders to put money, greed and control to one side and to understand that it means nothing, for what is the point of building empires, and acquiring untold riches when if things continue as they are, there will be no one left to enjoy it. If another Polar Shift takes place everything that has been created in your world will be destroyed.

Peace to you all.

Lazarus

CLEANSING AND PROTECTING GUIDE

This should be done every morning before getting out of bed. If you intend working with Spirit or have a job which creates a lot of negativity, then I cannot stress the importance of cleansing and protecting yourself.

By following this procedure, which only takes a minute when you become accustomed to it, it will stop any negative forces affecting your aura and will stop any negative entities becoming attached to you.

Sit quietly and make sure you will not be disturbed.

Step 1
Imagine a beam of pure vibrating white column of light about a foot above your head.

Step 2
Open crown chakra and allow white light to pass through your whole body. White light must exit through your feet into the ground. Repeat for 3 times.

Step 3

Imagine a red beam of grounding light coming up each foot, through each leg and then becoming one with white light in your heart centre.

Step 4
Allow the light to encompass your whole body, so it forms a protective bubble of white light over your head and under your feet.

Step 5
Imagine stepping into a hot air balloon and it carrying you up and up. If any cords attach from those on the earth plain, ask the angels to cut the ties with love, so you can soar as a free spirit.

Step 6
When you feel refreshed, come back down to earth gently and ask your angels and spirit guides to surround you with love and light and to keep you protected from any negativity.

MEET YOUR SPIRIT GUIDE MEDITATION

Imagine you are walking along a river bank on a glorious summers evening. You can hear children laughing and playing and hear the Midsummer's evening bird song. There is a gentle warm breeze and you feel peaceful and calm as you are gaze in wonder around you at the infinite beauty of nature. As you walk a little further along the bank you see a little boat moored to the side, get in and untie it, and allow yourself to drift along lazily basking in the summer's warmth and tranquillity.

You can trail your hand in the water as you drift by, and feel the calmness and peace embracing you as it washes away all your stress and negativity. A little ahead you see the opening to light airy woodland, where you tie your boat to the side and jump out and go gently in to the woodland. As you leisurely walk along the path in to the wood, notice what animals and insects you can see and hear, there may be deer frolicking in the grass, there may be rabbits hopping from place to place, there may be bees buzzing from one flower to another, gathering their pollen. Feel the peace and love and the beauty in this Mother Nature setting, you may see Sprites or Fairies or other earth spirits. You are in awe of what you can see, sense, feel and hear.

As you walk a little farther you can see a clearing up ahead and standing in the clearing is a little beautiful cottage with smoke coming from the chimney. As you walk up the cottage's path you can smell wood smoke mingled with honeysuckle and there are bluebells by the door. The door has been left ajar for you to go in. As you step inside you can feel nothing but love and welcome, and you know you are safe and loved in here. There are two armchairs by the open wood fire and in one of the armchairs is sat your Spirit Guide. Notice what they look like, ask them their name, and listen to what they have to tell you as they have been waiting to meet you for a long time. Feel free to ask them any questions you may have about your life, or in what way they can help you. Take the time to listen to their wisdom and guidance as they try to steer you to the right path in your life. Enjoy their company and feel the love from them encompassing all you do. When you have finished bid them farewell and give thanks for all you have learned, safe in the knowledge you can see them again whenever you choose.

Walk back up the path to where you left your boat, gently untie it and then make your way back up the river to where you first found the boat. Tie it back up and walk back up the river bank, back to the here and now, and back in to the room.

Note:
You can use this meditation for meeting your Angel, Fairy, Deceased loved one, or indeed anyone you wish. Just replace the person sitting in the armchair.

Please leave a review of this book on Amazon.com

If you would like to contact Judith in connection with this book, or if you would like more information on the many ways she can help you, please e-mail her at;
judithh@virginmedia.com

Or you can contact her via her website or Facebook page.

Website: www.judithhindle.co.uk

Facebook: @JudithHindleOfficial

Please look out for future titles from Judith, and non-spiritual books written in her maiden name of Judy Miller.

Coming Soon…..

'Inside the Mind of a Child'

Written under the name of Judy Miller, this is the true story of the author's troubled childhood, and how all those who work with vulnerable children, could help them so much better if they truly understood what the children were *really* thinking….

Printed in Great Britain
by Amazon